The End Justifies the Pain : Writings About Mental Health

John Frederick Zurn

Published by Everlasting Light, Yorkville, IL, 2022.

The End Justifies the Pain
: Writings about Mental Health
by John Frederick Zurn
© Copyright May 2022
All rights reserved
Cover page photo by Samantha Sophia courtesy of Unsplash.com[1]

Everlasting Light Publishing Yorkville, IL USA

The names and locations of the facilities are actual places.

The people mentioned are real; however, their names have been changed to respect their privacy - with the exception of my wife Donna.

---

1.   https://unsplash.com/photos/l4RL-cUDrdI

Table of Contents

Preface

For over forty years, I have been seriously challenged by a mental illness. After about seven of those years, I began to gradually find my way. I have written a number of books about my experiences that I have quoted in *The End Justifies the Pain*, but I have also written poems, short stories, and several young adult fantasy novels.

Several years ago, I began doing presentations for NAMI of DuPage (The National Alliance on Mental Illness), and during that time I gave about four hundred presentations. The presentations include a wide variety of audiences: hospitals, nursing schools, police departments and university students. In addition to formal presentations, I am consistently asked about my experiences by relatives and acquaintances. Some people talk to me about their "friends" that are having difficulties.

Because of the continuing interest in my ideas, I decided to better communicate my thoughts and to larger audience. To be honest, sharing my challenges with others has been some of the most meaningful experiences of my life. One of the main objectives of this book collection, *The End Justifies the Pain* is to give something back for all the mental health professionals, relatives, and friends who have been so vital to my learning to live with my bipolar disorder. Finally, I'd like to thank my wife, Donna, and my older brother Bernie, not only for their hard work and support in creating this book, but also for their inspiration and support over a lifetime.

Introduction

As the title *The End Justifies the Pain* suggests, the following pages assert that mental illness can be very difficult to diagnose and yet, at the same time can lead to a unique form of awareness that transcends the limitations of simply "treading water." Like the Phoenix recreating itself from the ashes, an individual struggling with a serious mental illness can overcome the many obstacles that limit substantive potential and purpose.

As an individual with a diagnosis of bipolar disorder, I have spent most of my life coping with an illness that is very difficult to identify and often extremely challenging to manage. For me, and millions of others, this illness continues to defy any comprehensive explanation, and for most of us; recovery can be a lifelong process. Even as medications continue to improve making life better for many, the illness itself has no known cure. This dilemma has left many of us who cope with bipolar disorder feeling healthy enough to function, but still sick enough to face recurring symptoms. Over the years, we have undergone any number of treatments in hospitals and other mental health settings seeking relief and the promise of long-term recovery. With the vital help of mental health professionals, family, friends and our own perseverance, many of us have diligently worked for a chance to live a life of purpose with a renewed sense of inner strength and courage.

In the following pages I will describe some of my personal experiences and a number of concepts that have made a normal life possible for me. In addition, I will share some creative stories and poems that reflect my thoughts and feelings as I have matured.

The major story in the first chapter is an autobiography. It represents a factual and truthful experience of my early years. These experiences are sometimes embarrassing; however, I believe telling the truth is a more accurate and useful way to describe them.

I also suspect these experiences show how important it has been for me to develop a sense of self-discipline. This includes developing an authentic sense of self-esteem and discovering realistic attitudes in terms of work routines, and medications. Essentially, writing has helped me clarify my impressions and experiences, so I can better integrate them into my life.

These various ideas and feelings that I have come to trust are the things that have worked for me over many years. These concepts and attitudes are now a kind of internal structure that helps me in day-to-day living. They also have proven invaluable in my relationships with others.

In the next three chapters are a lengthy discussion about medications, coping skills, and creativity as seen through the eyes of an individual with bipolar disorder. These chapters attempt to discuss, in some detail, my personal perspective on long-term recovery, and my belief in the power of creativity. These chapters can be approached as a kind of reading smorgasbord. If readers find some ideas useful, but others, not so much, I encourage them to investigate the appropriate concepts throughout the section. At the end of each chapter is a summary that reviews each section, and includes additional ideas and activities.

The fifth chapter contains two short stories called, "Uriel Fox and the Nursing Home Tragedy" and "The Secret Suffering of the Mentally Ill." Both stories are true, in fact, with some added creative influences to make them more accessible. Although these experiences occurred a long time ago, both are essentially accurate historical accounts that still point out the struggle of those of us with a mental illness. I also suspect that some experiences still exist that are similar to the ones in these stories.

The poems in the final chapter are my most personal writings reflecting on my own thoughts and feelings at any given time. While highly subjective, they represent some general emotions and understanding of individuals with bipolar disorder. Some of these ideas in the poems have evolved over time, but most of them reflect my personal struggle over the years.

Chapter 1 : MEMOIRS

Ridgeway Hospital

In some ways, this isn't a story about me at all. Instead, it's the story of an old friend of mine, who has stayed with me like a half-forgotten memory over the years. He's a good companion in a lot of ways, and he has helped me through some very difficult times. But truth be told, he has a little of the rebel in him. He's unpredictable, sometimes surly, and generally has the knack for making people feel uncomfortable. Whether he has changed over the last few years and turned some corner in his life, I can't say. But fond memories often drift through my mind whenever I remember our time together.

Yet, despite our friendship, I've often tried to "ditch" him because he continually seems to get me into some kind of trouble. After a while, he crosses some line or breaks some rule, and then, inevitably, a crisis erupts. So, eventually, I always desert him and find my own way. By moving around and leaving no forwarding address, my deepest hope has been for him to leave me alone.

But no matter how often I try to deceive him, he almost always appears at my front door complaining bitterly about my lack of gratitude for his many years of loyal friendship. So, after a few moments of awkward silence, I have always ended up apologizing, and we then usually rummage through the past and slug down martinis.

Now you see, once again I've ditched him, and he seems to be gone for good. His name is Robert Porter, but I just call him Bob. My name is John.

Of course, there is really no way of telling Bob's story without telling my own because we often worked, played, and struggled as one. Over the years, whenever we were together, we worked at a lot of minimum wage jobs that were often nasty and tedious. Perhaps that was one of the reasons we got into so much trouble during those years.

The drudgery of factory work and the constant demands of fast food restaurant customers made it hard to stay sober for long.

Still, there was one kind of trouble that Bob and I just couldn't seem to avoid. Any time we hung out together, Bob almost always ended up with mental health issues. Throughout our relationship, I watched him become ill repeatedly, and he often dragged me down with him. Because of this unstable situation, we were often forced to live in temporary placements as we coped with the day-to-day problems of living.

Yet, in these same unconventional circumstances, Bob and I often learned about the thoughts and feelings of others as well as our own. Whenever we were with other patients and residents, we almost always learned something about life.

So, in some ways, Bob was also a kind of blessing for me as well. He led me to people and places I would never have found without him. So, this story is not just about Bob and me, it is also a story about those fellow sojourners who crossed our path.

The triggering event that set my whole story in motion was an acute appendicitis attack when I was twenty. By the time I had surgery, I was in serious trouble. I woke up in the recovery room with no complications, but the fear of death soon became an obsession.

Over the next few years, this fear of death began to spread through my consciousness and poison my relationships. Every day brought only meaningless work and boredom. At night, the loneliness and despair were as palpable as a foul breeze. Before long I was severely depressed.

When I first met Bob, we were both patients at a private hospital called Ridgeway. I was there for depression, and Bob was there for being completely incoherent. When I first saw him, he was tied in a hospital bed with his thoughts racing so fast that his speech was wild and unintelligible. But slowly, as I watched him over the next few days and nights, I heard him slow down his speech although the words were still crooked and broken. After about a week, as my depression began to lift, I noticed Bob pacing around the unit. I decided to follow him; I also decided to take a good look around.

Ridgeway Hospital was a modern facility with clean, bright hallways honeycombed with double occupancy rooms. There was a dayroom that was also a dining room, several psychiatrists' offices and both an art and group therapy room. Adjoining the day room was the prominent nurses' station, the central hub of the entire hospital unit.

Patients wandered up to the chest high counter to take medications, find out about relatives, and often just to get attention. Most of the patients at Ridgeway were a mix of alcoholics, the seriously mentally ill, and drug addicts, so the atmosphere was sometimes frightening with an odd combination of staff cheerfulness and patient despair.

As I mentioned, Bob did get better by degrees at the hospital, and we soon became friends. Whenever we could, we met for meals and chatted during the day. We also talked about finances and discussed the possibility of sharing an apartment. It wasn't long before I trusted him as a loyal companion. Since I didn't make friends easily anymore, I felt really encouraged.

Anyway, since we were "new," we observed as much as we participated; but as Bob became more lucid, he also seemed more self-confident. He was more eager than I was to get involved and before long, he was giving advice. For example, at a morning group therapy session, he listened intently to a woman who was almost catatonic.

Somewhere, lodged within her struggling mind, she had come to believe that she had committed the Bible's "unforgivable sin." The tangled rollers in her hair and her food-stained nightgown painted a portrait of fear and despair. She really seemed to believe that she was going to hell. Sadly, Bob couldn't resist the temptation to talk to her about other relevant Bible passages suggesting that the woman could be helped. Unfortunately, Bob's enthusiasm sounded more like anger than compassion, so the group moved on.

Later, in the same group, Bob also engaged a heroin dealer in a heated discussion about the man's future. The man, who was taking methadone, told the group that he had decided to stop taking heroin himself, but would still sell it to others. Bob responded with a kind of mini-lecture that nearly deteriorated into a fist fight. For a time after that, Bob kept his opinions to himself.

Knife Fight

After the incidents in group, Bob was assigned many alternate activities that allowed him more freedom of expression. Bob participated in art therapy, wrote stories on typing paper, and went on community outings. As he became more coherent, we were both allowed more chances to become independent, and Bob seemed somewhat less argumentative.

But Bob was still sometimes quarrelsome with other patients and even staff. In fact, whenever a challenging situation developed, he was usually right in the middle of it. He didn't seem to mind the unpredictability of the other patients and the intensity of chaotic situations. So, while I spent much of my time reading through hospital magazines and comforting withdrawn patients who tried to hide in their rooms, Bob kept busy settling arguments, some of his own making.

Whenever a patient needed to be escorted to his room for throwing a chair or pushing over a table, it was Bob who often witnessed the event. If a patient tried to escape through the unit door when a staff member was leaving, Bob might suggest to him to "follow the rules." His assertive personality and careful attention to the behavior of others made him an unpredictable character, who was unable to see his own faults at times.

Not surprisingly, Bob often became energized by these tense, often unpredictable, situations. He appeared to be genuinely inspired and exhilarated by participating in all kinds of intense situations. And if Bob was overzealous sometimes, he usually had good intentions. On balance, he probably did no real harm either.

As for me, because I wasn't very ill, I was more intimidated and overwhelmed by these aggressive episodes. It was the unexpected slamming of doors and frequent screaming matches that so jangled my nerves and drained my strength. The day-to-day struggle to remain focused and balanced was often very difficult for me. Although, after a while, I did become more confident and assertive, and Bob flourished. While my self-confidence gradually improved, I still lacked Bob's daring and impulsive nature.

Although Bob and I both benefited from our first hospital experience, after we returned to "the world," it wasn't long before we had our first major falling out, so to speak. Some of the details are vague, but the basic facts are still clear in my mind.

It happened one night after work, while Bob and I were watching some boring TV soap opera repeat. (It was the typical drama - same characters, same plot, same commercials, same dialogue, etc.) I was really tired of watching it, so I turned the channel and suggested we had had enough reruns at Ridgeway.

Bob, however, must have taken my remark the wrong way. He grabbed a knife from the coffee table and began taunting me with it, half-seriously. When I jumped behind the couch, he tripped over the coffee table and accidentally stabbed himself in the chest. He rolled over on his back and fainted. I stood there stunned for a few moments, and then composed myself enough to dial 911. The dispatcher instructed me not to move him and specifically told me not to pull out the knife. When the ambulance arrived, the paramedics rushed Bob to the hospital, where, after surgery, he was recovering in intensive care.

Although Bob would completely recover, the damage to our relationship was not repairable. He simply could not accept that he was responsible for the accident. In fact, bizarre as it sounds, he blamed me for the entire incident and accused me of provoking him. So, even though I was truly grateful that Bob was okay, the entire situation was so intense and frightening that I decided to "ditch" him completely and make a new start. I thought that I would never see him again. I thought we had parted for good. But I was wrong.

Driving Under An Influence

Having moved to an entirely different metropolitan area, I felt sure that Bob wouldn't have any idea where to find me. I covered my tracks pretty well, and began looking for work again. I felt confident and optimistic as I walked toward the mega mall with my resume folded neatly in my coat pocket.

But as I was walking down the snowy sidewalk, a green Chevy Nova pulled over to the curb and someone inside asked me if I wanted a ride. I opened the car door, and before I knew what was happening, I was in the car with Bob.

We were both stunned initially; I felt trapped and speechless. But, then I was able to conjure up a hasty explanation about my disappearance, based on my sick aunt who had recently died. At first, Bob seemed to believe me, but as we drove on, he began to find flaws in my "dead relative" alibi and got really angry. He became disoriented and punched the gas pedal to the floor, racing through stop signs and ignoring traffic lights. The car swerved all over the road nearly hitting other vehicles.

Before long an angry legion of police squad cars were pursuing us into the mega mall parking lot. With one last acceleration, Bob rammed his Nova into a snow bank. Then an officer immediately jumped out of his squad car, smashed Bob's front window and dragged us both out of the car. After we were handcuffed, I looked over at Bob and saw him muttering something about friends always betraying each other. As we were driven to the police station, I was confused and very frightened.

When we were being fingerprinted at the front desk, I was too scared to explain myself properly. The only excuse I could come up with centered on my being merely a hitchhiker looking for a ride to the mall. The police, however, were not persuaded. They didn't believe that Bob and I were in the same car because of some odd set of coincidences. Bob also eagerly supported the police version of events that stated we had been friends for many years, and that I had actually called Bob for a joyride. Probably the police believed Bob, because it was the safest way to arrest both of us and so keep us both in custody.

During the entire interrogation process, Bob seemed oblivious to the situation. He playfully joked with the officers, and they seemed less tense than earlier at the mall parking lot. Of course, he ignored me completely, but I was so disoriented that I wasn't interested in talking with anyone.

Later, as we were being unloaded at the acute ward of Elgin State Hospital, I felt a sinking feeling in my soul, that my hopes and dreams were slowly unraveling.

Elgin State Hospital

The only reason Bob and I were in a locked ward at a state hospital instead of in a county jail cell was because Bob hadn't hurt anyone. But, believe me, Elgin State Hospital was nothing like our first hospitalization at Ridgeway either. The long dimly lit corridors with their faded linoleum floors were dreary and dirty. Cigarette butts were scattered everywhere on the floor, and an atmosphere heavy with anxiety smothered the spirit and withered the heart.

The men were separated from the women by a metal door that led to one of the men's day rooms. This door was opened three times a day for meals. The men also had a huge common dormitory where they all slept. It was locked all day, every day, except on Sundays when it was opened a few extra hours in the morning. There were also a counselor's room, another common room, and a shower area.

Because almost nobody had their own clothes, they were made available at night. They looked ratty and were often missing pockets, buttons, and zippers, but the patients made do. The one quirk in the system was the showers. They were open eighteen hours a day; so some of the patients took showers repeatedly, in an effort to escape from their problems and relax.

Another imposing area of the acute ward was the nurses' station. Unlike Ridgeway hospital, it wasn't the central focus of the entire ward, and it was much better fortified. A reinforced glass window surrounded the entire station except for the front, where patients, who wanted to smoke, were given a single wooden match that had to be struck in the staff's presence. Since very few relatives called and because the staff was usually inaccessible, no one lingered at the station for long, except to line up when medications were given out.

One of the strangest things about the acute ward was the two TV sets that were bolted on the ceiling in both the common room and in the hallway. They were always on, but never worked. All they ever did was produce endless static. As we patients paced up and down the halls all day, the odd noise and flip-flipping grated on our nerves and probably helped feed into our delusions and paranoia.

It was in this deeply dysfunctional hospital that Bob and I were forced to live for a time. Since we were stuck there for a while, I tried to become "unremarkable" so I wouldn't have to socialize and get involved with other people. Bob, however, undertook the self-appointed task of social director. He cheered up patients who were struggling and often gave advice. He sometimes met patients in the bathroom where they brewed tap water coffee. Bob also helped them scavenge the hall for cigarette butts that were later recycled.

Before moving on, I'd like to write a little more about the common sleeping area because it is the setting for one of Bob's more interesting antics. Since the dormitory was locked all day, the patients were forced to sleep on the floor in the hallway. This behavior was discouraged by staff, especially during inspections, but it was probably inevitable for the twenty or so patients who were always drowsy from boredom, medication or both.

But, leave it to Bob to find a way around the rules. Over the course of a week, Bob observed that when a patient "acted up," he was either put in restraints or received a thorazine (tranquilizer) injection in the lower hip. The restraints were used for the more dangerous situations and involved being loosely tied, spread-eagled in a bed for a few hours. However, Bob also discovered that the injection meant a free trip to the community sleeping room where the patients could stay in a bed all day and "sleep it off."

So, one morning Bob and Mike hatched a plan to get an injection. Mike was a long-term repeater who got his social security check each month and then got himself discharged. He then spent all his money and returned to the institution, usually in a few days.

Together, Bob and Mike picked their moment and shoved over a huge filing cabinet. It made a terrible, crashing sound as it hit the floor.

Staff came running and soon the nurse appeared - right on schedule, so to speak, and ordered the staff to escort Bob and Mike to the nurses' station. She gave them the "dreaded" shot, and they were taken to the common sleeping room where they slept the entire day.

However, Bob and Mike's strategy worked for only a short time. Once the nurse understood the game and figured out the purpose of the behavior, she abruptly changed the consequences. Their next disturbance left Bob in restraints for several hours. He and Mike then gave up on their injection idea, and Bob returned to his daily routine of tap water coffee, cigarette recycling, and newspaper interpretation.

I was not nearly as optimistic, mischievous, and clever as Bob. I mostly sat around in the dining area and eventually began to pick up writing. With nothing to do but eat, sleep, and pace, I needed to occupy my mind. I wrote mostly about myself in imaginary places doing nonsensical deeds. Surprisingly, the staff always seemed willing to give me pencils and paper; so I wrote almost daily, either early in the morning or late in the evening. During these times, it was usually pretty quiet.

Despite my growing depression and feelings of isolation, I still remained determined to persuade the psychiatrists to discharge me. I was also becoming gradually convinced that Bob was a bad influence on my character, and that he was possibly mentally unstable, so I tried my best to avoid him.

It is helpful to describe the discharge system at Elgin State Hospital to help inform the reader about the mental health system and the patients' problems coping with it. This system of patient management is simple to understand, but difficult to master.

The first step was to earn a pass to leave the ward and walk the grounds. This required a psychiatrist's signature with staff approval. This pass privilege was sometimes used as a kind of threat to keep patients in line, but it also served as a reminder that helped patient's better monitor their own behavior.

This pass was more valuable than might appear at first glance. The grounds were expansive and included: a commissary store, library, recreation center, chapel, medical and administrative buildings, and even a fire station. The commissary sold mostly consumables like instant coffee, cigarettes, and candy. The library lent out donated books and magazines. The grounds, themselves, had lots of evergreen trees and fields. As long as the patients didn't attempt to escape or explore boarded up buildings on the grounds, they were left alone to sleep or walk around. Often this initial pass privilege lasted anywhere from a few minutes to several hours.

The next level of pass privilege involved a weekend visit or outing. For this pass, there was a higher degree of behavioral scrutiny and included patient cooperation and symptoms management. Since the pass usually involved relatives, patients who were abandoned received help from the social workers. If the patient had nowhere to go, they were steered toward halfway houses and group homes for possible future placement. Sometimes a very generous church group or individual family might consider helping as well.

The final level, of course, was the discharge itself. This required overcoming all kinds of obstacles, such as lingering legal problems, homelessness, and employment issues. Almost always, these challenges created an anxious intensity in the minds of patients. The ones who really wanted to leave would repeatedly rehearse their pleas before they talked with the psychiatrists and counselors. They also made every effort to control their temper and behave "appropriately" even when encountering the most difficult patients.

All morning long, these patients would camp outside the locked door where the entire staff would be deciding their future. When the staff finished their meeting and eventually stepped into the hall, the psychiatrists would be surrounded by these anxious patients with their one desperate question: "Am I being discharged?"

Discharge And Return

As the days passed, I began to regret my attitude toward Bob. Although it was true that he often got me in trouble, he was also an exciting person to hang around with. In the early days, we had frequented bars and generally enjoyed the night life. Even back then, Bob attracted others with his infectious personality that seemed to attract all kinds of interesting people who were eager to draw on his positive energy. But beyond all that, Bob had been my friend for many years, and, as I've mentioned, I didn't make friends easily. My introverted nature and monotonous routines left me constantly frustrated and lonely. It became clear to me that, without Bob, I was a "nobody."

So, one morning after breakfast, I synchronized my pass time with Bob's. As he approached the commissary, I caught up with him and meekly apologized. At first, he was angry, but before long, he was able to sense my sincerity. By the time we had purchased our cigarettes and instant coffee, we were friends once more. I also realized that day, that Bob was my salvation, despite his faults and odd behavior. In the end, he was the only person who really stuck with me, no matter what.

Bob and I had a difference of opinion regarding medications. Bob had long been completely against taking them, because they made him feel drowsy and left his mouth dry. He also complained that the meds gave him an uncontrollable sensation that he described as "ants crawling around under his skin." He said this made it impossible for him to sit for any length of time. Truth be told, probably the only reason Bob swallowed the pills at all was because the nurses ordered him to open his mouth and roll his tongue around to make sure the pills all went down.

Yet, I suspect Bob disliked the medications for a few less obvious reasons as well. As a rule, they left him feeling lethargic, irritable, and unenthusiastic. In the end, Bob also believed, I think, that taking the medications were a sign of weakness and demonstrated a lack of faith.

Bob's self-confidence was threatened by their purpose and effects, so he never stuck with them for long.

Even though for the most part I agreed with Bob about the medications, I was more indifferent than antagonistic. I just took them, and didn't even bother to ask the nurse about them. When I eventually reached the front of the medication line, I just took the pills, three times a day. I do vividly recall, however, that the patients all looked like zombies as they passed me in the hallways. I remember wondering if I was watching them or if I was one of them myself.

Anyway, Bob and I were ready for discharge after a couple of months. I had helped Bob stay out of trouble, and he was good at keeping me busy; so the staff figured out a way to shuffle our paperwork and optimize our histories, so to speak. Thankfully, a Christian couple took us in and made us part of their home and church community. We acquired work at a local department store and lived in genuine contentment for a number of months. I also, persuaded Bob to take the medications by fabricating some idle threats about our relationship and what would happen if he went off them.

But, as usual, Bob had other ideas. He discreetly flushed his meds down the toilet, three times a day, and things deteriorated quickly. He began drinking, even in the morning, and his behavior started to slip, creating a sense of urgency on the part of the church leaders. The group rightly explained to us that Bob was "out of fellowship" and that we needed to leave the church community immediately.

With no particular place to go, Bob and I began roaming around the streets of downtown Elgin. We begged for beer money during the day, and at night we camped outside a local Mexican restaurant until closing time. Sometimes the workers gave us leftover tacos and burritos.

The wildest thing I remember during those weeks happened at 6 a.m., when Bob and I walked up to a bar filled with construction workers. Bob sauntered up to a huge man who had a gun in one hand and a big wad of cash in the other. Bob said something sarcastic to the man and soon the barrel of the gun was pointing at Bob's head. I instinctively screamed, and Bob followed my lead. By the time we reached the corner, the man was laughing wildly. Apparently, he had lowered his weapon long before we stopped running.

Yet, I really did like having Bob around again, despite the awkward moments and occasional "close calls." The adventure and excitement that I felt at times was far superior to my monotonous life of daily responsibilities. The tedious routine and mind-numbing relationships were left far behind, as Bob created endless possibilities for fame and fortune. Every moment became electric, with new opportunities to create a tapestry of exciting experiences.

Bob also helped me understand the deeper, more hidden connections in our lives, like the secret way of numbers, and the prediction of events. Bob even helped me piece together magazines, newspapers, and street signs to reveal secret messages about famous people. I then understood very clearly that I stayed with Bob because he was a pilgrim and a chronic explorer.

Still, Bob's desire to explore had unforeseen consequences at times. He got so enthusiastic during our time on the street, that he whispered to me, that he was Jesus. Now, I know how crazy that sounds, but it was more of a misinterpretation than the mutterings of an unbalanced person. Besides, Bob had mentioned Jesus often before, but not as openly as during those weeks.

As you may have already guessed, Bob told the wrong person about his "secret identity" and we were back in the state hospital the next evening. Since I had already decided that I wouldn't leave Bob again, I did my own Jesus impersonation and they took us both together.

Altogether, Bob and I were patients in Elgin State Hospital three different times. Rather than getting bogged down in a lot of repetitive details, I will focus on a few important incidents that occurred during our last two hospital stays. These events reveal some important details about other patients, and also help shed light on Bob's personality, and in so doing, perhaps reveal something of my own as well.

The first incident concerns a long-term patient who had been given some medications that caused his tongue to stick out of his mouth continually. Worse yet, he constantly bit it, so he kept a saliva and blood-soaked towel against his chin at all times, even at meals. This situation steadily worsened for a couple of weeks. During this time, Bob and I took turns reassuring him by telling him not to worry because "God will take care of you." After a few weeks, the psychiatrists finally figured out a way to help him, and the patient's tongue retreated back into his mouth. The patient immediately sought us out and mimicked our statement that "God will take care of you."

The man's stinging remark struck me like a thunderbolt. Clearly, God was *not* helping him, or any of us for that matter. Although Bob shrugged off the patient's sarcastic remark, I was more reflective and realized that "blind faith" didn't work for us.

For me, it wasn't a matter of believing in God or not. It was more the idea that I had to take responsibility for my own life, and not rely on others to "fix me." After that self-reliance became as important as faith for me.

A more tragic, incident that Bob and I both witnessed occurred in stages and played out over our three extended hospital stays at Elgin. During our first stay, we saw a woman, I'll call her Mary, who was in the commissary seating area. She was wearing a torn, filthy dress, and she had coffee grounds on the corners of her mouth. She also had a fly swatter and was swinging at imaginary flies.

The next time we saw Mary, we were astonished to see her completely transformed. She had on a bright spring jumper, her hair was beautifully blonde, and her face was radiant. She spoke "normally" to others at the commissary, and appeared genuinely happy.

But the last time Bob and I were hospitalized at Elgin, Mary was about six months pregnant. She had returned to former state of misery.

She had coffee grounds all over her face, and she was swinging the fly swatter again. When Bob and I saw her, we were stunned. It was such a horrible sight that Bob and I have often talked about her over the years.

A less intense incident took place while Coleman and I were waiting for a shower to open up. I knew Coleman pretty well, and we sometimes walked the grounds together. While we were waiting our turn in the shower area, Coleman turned to me and asked me if I had swallowed any milk at dinner. When I didn't answer, he told me that it had LSD in it, and that now he was hallucinating.

For some reason, that brief look into Coleman's mind had not been revealed to me until that moment. It gave me yet another reason to remain friends with Bob. At least I could understand him, most of the time.

Hell

As I mentioned earlier, Bob and I left Elgin State Hospital for good on our third try. We eventually returned to college, now and then, and we sometimes worked at minimum wage jobs. But Bob was never one to stay in one place for long. He yearned for a real education beyond the ivory towers and factory dungeons.

So, one day, just for the thrill of it, we engaged a cab for two hundred and fifty dollars and traveled downstate to visit a friend who was studying at a major university. When we arrived, Bob and I realized that our expectations far exceeded the reality of our reception. Our friend was busy studying and declined our poorly timed suggestion to get drunk, especially since it was the middle of the afternoon on a weekday. When we left him an hour later, we were basically stranded.

Because Bob and I had squandered all our cash on cab fare, we were forced to seek the help of a university counselor, so we could get out of town. Bob, who had been literally sucking broken glass seeking "hidden" help, was persuaded to follow me to the counselor's office. Luckily, the counselor was able to find us enough money to put us on a bus to Chicago.

When we boarded the bus, we sat directly behind the bus driver, and then sang Elvis songs for the whole trip. By the time we arrived at the Chicago bus station, it was late evening and we were really flying high, so to speak. Then, as we began our trek down a Chicago city street, Bob had one of his compelling revelations.

As we quickened our pace, Bob revealed to me that the British rock group *Wings* was giving a concert in Chicago that very night! Our "mission" was to direct traffic, so people could get in. Then, we were going to join the group members off stage after the show. Although I was really surprised to hear Bob describe this exciting situation, he had been right before. So, I decided ignore my doubts and inhibitions and began helping him.

The first thing Bob did was to take out his expired draft card and ceremoniously burn it. Next, he removed his shoes and began walking down the middle of the street. Since it was getting late, there wasn't much traffic, and the cars pulled around us easily. Bob then took out his wallet and unstitched it. He also re-stitched it, so it would hang from his neck like the front of a criminal mug shot.

As we continued our journey down the street, Bob removed his belt and began whipping cyclone fences by the sidewalks. When the furiously growling, junkyard guard dogs attacked the fence, Bob struck the fence with his belt even harder.

By about 2 a.m., Bob decided to finish his mission. He suddenly halted in the middle of the street and had me help him block traffic completely. At first, the traffic ignored us. But then a semi-truck stopped in front of us, blocking the street in both directions. In the meantime, patrons of a nearby tavern began hurling empty beer bottles at us. One man ran up to Bob and threw him to the ground. He raised his fist, as if he were about to punch him directly in the face, but as he was about to strike, the man relented for some reason. Ten minutes later, Bob and I were in a police patrol car on our way to Cook County Jail.

When we arrived at the police station, it was frightening and chaotic. It felt like the middle of rush hour instead of the middle of the night. Police officers were racing around corners, criminals were pushed up against the walls and on the floor, and undercover officers were hustling through the mob of people. At first, I wasn't terribly anxious but that was soon to change

Since Bob and I were considered "squirrels," we were sent to the psych area of the prison called Cermak. As soon as we entered the building with the other prisoners, we were immediately ordered to "strip." Then the officers examined every orifice of our bodies for weapons and drugs. By the time we reached our psych floor, my mild anxiety had evolved into wild eyed terror. Bob, for once, appeared about as terrified as I was.

Some of the inmates, like Bob and me, were restrained on metal beds for about three days with one free hand for eating. Because we were tied in bed, the sheets had to be changed every day. Some of the police officers also looked the other way, when some prisoners, who were left unrestrained, were allowed to assault Bob and me whenever they wanted to. I'll never forget the time when a criminal came into our open cell while we were sleeping and tried to snap our necks. I heard the strangest cry of wild geese when my neck snapped back in place.

Finally, after a few horrifying days, the guards let us up, and after couple of more days, they escorted us to the front door. Then they simply pushed us out onto the street with no shoes or belts. As we walked down the sidewalk, holding up our pants with our hands, I thought that Bob and I were finally liberated from the jail for good. Although we had no idea where we were, we thought we were safe.

Unfortunately, because of a bizarre set of circumstances, our relationship to Cook County Jail was far from over. Several weeks later, when we were picked up at a movie theater for bothering patrons, the police scanner revealed that during our first incarceration at the jail, we had missed our court date for the Chevy Nova incident, so the police officer arrested us both again. This time, however, we were taken to the central jail and left there.

The inside of Chicago's Cook County Jail was different from the previous psych jail. Instead of individual cells, there was one huge common dormitory room with about thirty metal bed frames that were bolted to the floor. The guards stood at the front, where they constantly ran around breaking up fights. The showers were off to the side partially out of the guard's line of sight. Meals were served downstairs by various prisoners, and inmates sat at long steel tables. Near the dining hall were a number of individual cells reserved for trouble makers from both the dormitories and dining area.

The whole situation was dangerous, but the two most treacherous areas were the showers and the far end of the bed rows. I discovered these perils through observations and my own experience. Since Bob and I were initially assigned in the back, we realized before long that other prisoners could make and carry out threats without being seen. As unbelievable as this may sound, the exact same prisoner, who was imprisoned in the psych section of the jail, was now threatening to kill us again. When we freaked out, however, the guard moved us way up front.

The shower was yet another hazard that Bob and I had to deal with. Near the inside of the shower wall, just out of view, prisoners sometimes waited to attack other prisoners. We were taunted near there, so we avoided the shower area completely.

There were also other weird things going on, one of which involved Bob. Since the murderers were tossed in with the nonviolent criminals, things were really intense much of the time. One man attempted to fake appendicitis. Another tried to keep himself busy by making "orange peel hand lotion" wine. Still others stared blankly at the concrete walls. One person named Peter, smiled absently with an unchanging expression on his face. Both the inmates and guards assumed Peter's smile was sarcastic and directed at them. It wasn't, but they tried to "teach him a lesson" anyway.

As mentioned earlier, Bob sometimes did things that I am ashamed to report. One prisoner, with a noticeable eye astigmatism, for example, was constantly pacing in front near Bob's bed. Whenever the man looked at Bob, Bob would mockingly cross his own eyes. The guard never caught on, but the prisoner saw it every time. Finally, the man picked up a shoe and hit Bob over the head with it. Bob's head started bleeding, and the man was pushed into an individual jail cell with no discussion.

Then Bob did the strangest thing. He opened his Bible and wiped his head with it. He then sat absentmindedly like a person who couldn't bear reality any longer. Later, when I was allowed to accompany him to the infirmary, his head was sown up with a few stitches. I asked him about his bizarre behavior, and he told me he was trying to "get us the hell out of here."

But it was actually our Christian friends, Jan and Matt, who "got us the hell out of there." I persuaded Bob to let me call them, to see if they would bail us out. When I called them, they agreed to help us, and get us an attorney; however, Bob and I had to agree to pay them back.

Without their help, I dare not think what murderers or other vile circumstances might have ended our lives. And although I had come to believe that trusting myself was the most important thing to do, it was two deeply devout Christians who had rescued the both of us.

Zeller State Hospital

Bob and I did re-pay Jan and Matt for the loan that covered our bail and attorney. The attorney was very qualified and was able to satisfy the judge with "time served." But before long, the gratitude we both felt, began to fade, and the boredom of the Elgin area began to reassert itself. After a few months, we wandered down to the city of Peoria. I'm not really sure how or why Bob and I ended up in the state hospital there, but I do remember that we spent at least a couple of months there during the winter and spring.

Before describing this hospitalization, at Zeller State Hospital in Peoria, I want to describe the general conditions of the many situations in which Bob and I have been the central figures.

First, at Cook County Jail - Bob and I were there for about nine days in total. However, most of the inmates were trapped there for months at a time. The guards were also trapped there in a sense. Every day and night, they had to return and work in the same appalling environment as the prisoners. The chaotic situation was very dangerous for everyone. At one time, I often felt that County Jail was hell itself. While Bob and I were merely "passing through," many others were at the jail for an indeterminate amount of time; so, their circumstances were considerably worse.

Next, the hospitals - Bob and I were patients in those forsaken institutions for months at a time. Many of the patients, however, had been living there for years. These patients were considered "chronic." Either none of the medications they had been given really worked or the patients had just given up. Their lives were certainly much more difficult than ours, and they were probably not destined for a "happy ending."

Many staff members genuinely cared about the welfare of their patients, both "chronic" and "curable." Often, we patients were unruly and stubborn, yet the staff seemed to take each new day as it dawned.

In fact, in some ways, the staff and patients were almost like a surrogate family, which made all our lives bearable.

Finally, the historical context - Most of the stories about us took place in the 70s and 80s. This is important to remember. The state of mental health treatment has dramatically changed since then. New medications, important laws, and better facilities have eclipsed the antiquated systems Bob and I were exposed to all those years ago.

These events did actually happen. It is also a huge mistake to suggest that people suffering with mental illnesses are either always "cured" or somehow have it easier. One need only seek out the homeless or search the nursing homes to find people who are abandoned and suffering. Perhaps even the teen dropout next door is one of us "hiding in plain sight."

To continue the story... Bob and I had been dropped off at Zeller State Hospital around Christmas time. I'm sure that Bob must have had something to do with our admission, but, as I said, I don't remember.

However, I do remember some of the other people who were there, while Bob and I were patients there. I recall we were both in capable hands at Zeller and the place was pretty cheerful. To be more direct, the patients were really ill, but the environment was surprisingly enthusiastic.

Even though the hospital was supportive, Bob was pretty much "out there" again. He angered the German born psychiatrist immediately, by asking him who he fought beside during World War II. The psychiatrist responded by tossing Bob out of his office, and didn't really talk to him again, until I made Bob apologize a few weeks later.

During our time at Zeller, Bob also took a greater interest in TV and began watching inspiring religious shows. He often secretly waved to the preachers and watched other patients touch the TV screen. Bob sometimes "spoke in tongues" as well, but he only did it around me.

While Bob was busy "getting into himself," I began to learn a fair amount about compassion and courage. I finally acknowledged the genuine suffering of others, and became more understanding of their behavior. Unlike Bob, I began to realize that compassion was different than giving advice. So instead of getting "psychologically high" with Bob, all the time, I began to see that he and I weren't the only ones trying to make sense of our lives.

For example, there was a woman at Zeller who had been recently divorced from her husband. Because she couldn't accept it, she imagined that she was still married to him. In her confusion, she wore several different outfits at once and covered her face with makeup. She then would return to her room and change again, as if this would transport her back to the past. The staff tried gently to help her see the truth of the situation, but she wasn't able to listen.

Another patient in his late twenties was also unable to face the future. He was given a discharge from the armed forces, but he believed that as soon as he got out of the hospital, he would be able to reenlist, and pick up where he'd left off. His entire future was based on this mistaken premise. He talked about his plans, as if he were trying to convince himself.

Another person in distress was a patient named Will, who wasn't mentally ill at all. Whenever Will was first admitted, he would shriek out bizarre statements and wave his arms in the air, frightening everyone around him. Then, after his admission, he would simply eat and sleep a lot. One day I overheard a staff member say that Will was there for the "hundredth time." It turned out that Will was homeless and periodically needed a place to stay.

Despite all the misery, there were some good things about Zeller State Hospital. For example, the food tasted really good, and the whole place was clean. The staff was truly interested in the patients, even when they had to work during the Christmas holidays. Because of the staffs' attitude, the patients seemed less prone to frustration and aggression as well.

The best thing about Zeller was the sheltered workshop. With a building pass, patients could work for several hours a day gluing plastic medallions on red ribbons that were later attached to Kahlua bottles. The pay was determined by piecework, and it required patience and accuracy. Not only did the work pay cash, but it also helped relieve the suffocating boredom and helped break up the day. Although, Bob was faster at piecework than I was, he also had to fix a lot of mistakes. Still, both of us were able to earn enough money to pay for city bus fare, whenever we could earn an all-day pass.

It was on our return from one of these all-day passes, that Bob and I caught yet another glimpse of how the world sees mentally ill individuals. We were just stepping off of the city bus across from Zeller, when an obviously ignorant woman with a small child on her lap remarked, "That's where the crazy people live. They even have a crazy workshop!"

Ironically, the woman didn't know where Bob and I were going, but Bob was ready to jump back on the bus as it pulled away. I then remembered something a professor once said about all kinds of prejudices. He remarked that although a person might feel bad about their situation, at least they're better than "such and such group of people." Even though it was easy to see that the woman's comment was mostly harmless, it did remind me of the need to hide our identity. Generally, when anyone found out about our mental health issues, they never treated us the same again.

There was one other situation at Zeller that was particularly difficult to bear. Periodically, schools would take tours through the hospital. Invariably the tour group consisted of a number of co-eds with a football coach/gym teacher as chaperone. His job was to "protect" the students from us. These chaperones always looked worried as they hurried the students through the halls, making us feel like rabid animals. Sometimes, Bob would try to provoke the chaperones with the old "evil eye," but they just tried to ignore him.

Overall, the staff and counselors at Zeller State Hospital were extremely helpful. And it was there that Bob and I caught a real break. When we were discharged, the counselors set us up with a place to live and work that was guaranteed for a year.

Monroe House

It was after we had begun living at a facility called Monroe House, near downtown Peoria, that life began to markedly improve for Bob and me. For our part, we had agreed to follow all Monroe House rules, do chores, and attend all house meetings. This applied to all other six residents as well. In addition, we all agreed to work and treat each other respectfully at all times. If we kept all these agreements, we could stay at Monroe House for a year.

During the day most of us worked at the sheltered workshop a few miles away. At the workshop, Bob and I were assigned to work for Pamela, who supervised the food service department. We were all allowed to stay at the job training center for an indefinite period, and job counselors were there to help all of us find "real jobs" in the community.

Monroe House was ideal for Bob and me; it offered variety for Bob and a measure of security for me. I know making beds, setting tables, and doing dishes sounds boring. But for Bob, these chores provided an outlet for his incessant energy. He also enjoyed talking with the other six residents who were all on the rebound like us, or were trying to find some new purpose for their lives.

The counselors at Monroe House were all professionals with relaxed attitudes. They often had good ideas and suggestions. Bob and I both spent a lot of time with them and learned from their honesty and wisdom.

But, despite all of the counselors' help, the residents often had serious problems that were very difficult to solve. For example, a woman named Mary, who was the nicest, most compassionate person you're likely to meet, had somehow become attached to the idea that someone was trying to murder her. Although she was very well liked by everyone, she was consumed by this "prophecy of death." Mary held on to this belief consistently and apparently no counselor or friend could persuade her to believe differently. About six months later, Mary was actually murdered.

I believed, initially, that Mary had some psychic premonition about her death, and that no one believed her. However, I realized that she must have "deliberately" put herself in dangerous situations; maybe she was so depressed that she wanted to die. I suppose it doesn't really matter; dead is dead.

For some reason the counselors rarely discussed Mary's self-fulfilling prophecy. Maybe it was a privacy issue, or maybe they didn't want us to obsess over her. Either way, we still felt badly about Mary's tragedy.

June was another resident who died during her stay at Monroe House. June's circumstances were difficult to understand, and they include Bob and me as well. June became engaged and was planning to marry in about a year or so. Even though she had a bright future ahead of her, June suddenly refused to do her chores, or even go to work. She stayed in bed most of the day, apparently depressed.

The other residents grew impatient with June's "gold bricking" and began gossiping behind her back and even to her face. I stood by and said nothing, while Bob cursed under his breath and gave June timely advice about following the rules.

When June did finally go to the hospital, she was diagnosed with bone cancer. She was dead in less than a week. Everybody, including the counselors, was stunned. But the residents themselves were soon moving on to other issues. Perhaps, like me, they felt ashamed of themselves for the way they had treated June. Anyway, we all paid closer attention to chores and house rules. We all hoped to redeem ourselves, I suppose; or maybe we just wanted to forget. Moving on probably did work to some degree.

The other residents, including Bob and me, had problems of our own, but they were not life threatening. We had problems with anger, depression, medications, and alcohol, but we sometimes did better over time.

I met my good friend, Larry, while living at Monroe House during that year. Larry, Bob, and I went out drinking almost every night, but we managed to do all our chores and go to work consistently. We weren't supposed to be drinking, but the counselors chose to ignore it, making a "judgment call." I also began writing again every day and a glimmer of hope began to flicker.

Although we knew Larry for a number of years, he eventually told Bob and me that we needed to leave him behind. Because Larry's illness involved hearing voices, he felt our time together was slipping away. He believed two specific people from his past were constantly threatening him. Since medication didn't work and counseling didn't help either, Larry saw his situation as hopeless.

For example, one therapy Larry was given involved a rubber band attached to his wrist. Whenever he heard voices, he was instructed to snap the rubber band, thus breaking up the thoughts. I don't believe it ever worked very well; it seemed like prescribing an aspirin for a broken arm. But I never told Larry my opinion. I still think of Larry from time to time, The truth was we really couldn't take him with us. Sadly, he was probably right.

There was one unusual situation that evolved at Monroe House that was deeply troubling, yet very educational as well. It actually involved a female staff member and her ex-husband. Pat worked the overnight shift and almost always made herself available to residents as a counselor and a friend. We all adored her and considered ourselves fortunate to have her on staff.

However, Pat was also a person who would not be treated as a door mat either. When her ex-husband would come around a few nights a week, he was usually half drunk with a couple of beers dangling from his belt. Pat consistently refused to get back together with him. (This is, of course, a common-sense response.)

What made this situation so tragic was the ex-husband's recent diagnosis of multiple sclerosis. The disease had struck suddenly and moved quickly, and the man was devastated.

In bits and pieces, we residents learned about the situation, and if I recall the circumstances correctly, Pat's ex-husband had been cheating on her for a long, long time, until very recently. I also remember that she agreed to talk with him whenever he came to Monroe House. But she also refused to go back to him and she wouldn't be "guilted" into taking responsibility for his life.

As you might expect, Bob and I had different reactions to Pat's situation. Bob was interested in all the messy details, while I again saw that life is difficult for everyone regardless of appearances.

I must say that Bob, at times, did begin to take the world and his own life more seriously after all. Perhaps, the compassionate staff and close supervision of his medications, or maybe Bob's desire to find independence were important factors in his steady recovery.

Regardless, Bob began to write down his creative ideas instead of acting things out physically. He began to understand, I think, that creative behavior led only to negative consequences. It wasn't that Bob denied the validity of his ideas, he just began to see them as misunderstood by others and so potentially dangerous.

Naturally, I enthusiastically watched Bob's slow transformation into a more caring person. He was easier to talk with, and he began reading again. We spent time discussing psychology, religion, and literature. Of course, deep within, my ever-present fear was the same as it had always been. Will Bob stop taking the medication? By now, I was absolutely sure he needed it. But he wasn't nearly as sure as I was.

Overall, Monroe House was a great experience for Bob and me, although it would be an exaggeration to state that it was the entire reason for our recovery. The sheltered workshop in Peoria and our own self-effort were also instrumental in helping Bob and me become confident enough to return to a more traditional way of life.

While at the sheltered workshop, Bob and I worked with Pam in the food service department serving lunches, busing tables, and washing dishes. There were about twenty-five lunches to cook each day. Many other clients and staff brought their own lunches. They also used tables and dishes.

A few yards away from the main workshop area were different places (work lines) where physically and mentally challenged adults worked, almost exclusively on piecework jobs. The biggest problem on the work lines was, and continues to be, the lack of work. Even though workshops have a full-time sales representative, there is almost never enough work for any length of time. This creates disappointment and boredom for these workers who so badly want to work. Conversely, Bob and I were very fortunate because lunches were always served, regardless of the circumstances. We were also paid an hourly wage.

It was my counselor, Linda, who was responsible for getting Bob and me into the food service department. She was also the one who found the money for tuition and expenses, so we could return to the university. Without her support and encouragement, there would have been no money for school, and a very different future would have emerged. Sometimes, one person can make such a difference.

Surprisingly, Bob didn't want to return to the university. He told me that he was bored and restless. He just wanted to "coast for a while" as he put it. I was saddened by his decision, but I was okay with it. In the past, it had always been me who left him, so I felt guilty and deceitful. But now Bob was actually "ditching" me and that felt very different. With a clear conscience, I could say goodbye to Bob, perhaps never to see him again. When we both agreed to "keep in touch" with each other. I knew we were just saying the words with no conviction. We separated and went our own ways. I went back to school, and Bob journeyed out to see more of his world.

A Mystical Experience

When I returned to the university, it felt like I was finally home. The campus buildings, with their oddly scattered arrangement and unique designs, seemed to wait expectantly for the students to come scurrying into their classrooms. The students themselves seemed strangely familiar with their backpacks flung over their shoulder and their animated conversations. Before long, I too joined their ranks on the sidewalks and in the campus activity center. It was in this promising setting, that I renewed my studies in British and American literature.

When I first returned to my classes, I had trouble sitting down, because I was so genuinely excited. The prose and poetry of "the great ones" again afforded the opportunity to glimpse into a world of ideas and feelings that I had almost forgotten. Reading Coleridge's poem "Kubla Khan" suggested an inspirational power I could sense once more, even if I couldn't totally understand it. Blake's poem "The Tyger" seemed wild and strange, vaguely appealing. Even literary interpretations of these poems were saturated with mystery and power.

Equally alluring, were the lives of the authors themselves. Fighting their own personal demons, these authors expressed the possibility of art as a way to exorcise their doubts and deepest fears. By learning about their lives and beliefs, I could attempt to understand their life's journey through the uncertainties of human existence.

After a while, it became clear to me that some writers found a measure of peace in their lives, while others clearly did not. Perhaps the most unsettling discovery of all - throughout all my years of literary study - was the unpredictability and inevitability of death. Whether death came early to poets like Keats and Shelley, or if death was more obliging and patiently waited as in the life of Mark Twain; it arrived all the same.

It was the search for knowledge that so captivated me. During my time at the university, studying was a continuous process. While

"

walking to class, studying at the library, or jogging around campus, I lived in a world of ideas. Like so many other serious students, I was eager to find out life's meaning beyond just preparing for a career. Quizzes, tests, and research papers often became important strategies that helped internalize information and expand ideas. Dedicated professors fueled this need to grow with a dedication that sometimes felt like inspiration. By the end of the semester, I had earned a B.A. in English, and a graduate assistantship for the next academic year.

In the summer of 1980 after earning my B.A. degree, I experienced a life changing event that forever altered my beliefs about literature and life. Ever since Peoria, I had begun to meditate in a desperate attempt to control my thoughts. While diligently studying a book called *Journey of Awakening* written by Ram Dass, a former Harvard professor, I began to practice a simple meditation for twenty minutes a day.

Within a month I noticed, to my astonishment and relief, that my thoughts were beginning to slow down and even dissolve. As I gradually increased the duration of each session, thoughts became more and more peaceful. I continued this meditation practice and also became a student of Eastern philosophy. I also began jogging every day while counting my steps one to eight. Eventually, I even gave up drinking during this time.

During that summer, I was studying Mark Twain and his novels. Our professor, Dr. Josic, was such an inspiring lecturer, that by the time we began reading *The Mysterious Stranger*, I could sense a potent energy pulling me from deep within. After class one day, I went back to my campus apartment and began to meditate deeply. As the thoughts dissolved, I could feel the excitement of some presence directing and controlling my energy.

"I" sojourned beyond the sense of self, into a dark void, more vast than space itself. Then "I" apprehended the passage into death. With a final push, which can only be described as grace, "I" heard a beautiful bell sound, and then exploded into Light. This Light is not the physical light of science described so coldly and objectively, but rather an infinite Light Energy that is Love itself. This eternal Love-Light-Energy is Pure Being and indivisible into "parts."

During the few brief moments that I was in that chaotic, infinite energy, there was no sense of the world at all. There was also no sense of "I" or "me." Then I was "kicked back out"; my body convulsed and I struggled, trying to breathe. Finally, I was able to drink a glass of water, and slowly came around.

This transforming experience left no doubt about the existence of God for me. God as pure Love-Light-Energy was then, and continues to be, how I understand God within and behind creation. Like two sides of the same coin, God exists everywhere. I couldn't wait to tell Bob, if I ever saw him again. I felt certain meditation would bring him peace and slow his restless nature, perhaps as much as medicine did.

Yet, this truly wonderful experience did not have the effect on my life that the reader might suppose. In so many places, I have read that when one finds God, all problems are solved. Certainly, the deep inner yearning to find God had been resolved at last. But it also created a number of serious problems that I could never have anticipated.

First, since my whole reason for studying literature was to find out about God, once I had the "God Experience," I no longer had any interest in literature at all. Even more disturbing, there was no one to help me integrate this experience into my day-to-day routine. I wandered from class to class, trying to explain my discovery to professors in the English department. As one professor put it, "I left no stone unturned." Although they were very, very patient, they could not understand me. So, in the end, I started making connections and interpretations that left me vulnerable and alone.

Just as I was sinking into a sea of loneliness and despair, who should turn up at my door but Bob! Having looked my name up in the student directory, he knew right where to locate me. For the first time in our lives, Bob actually looked and sounded better than I did. He asked how

I was doing at school, and I tried my best to explain the whole "God situation." I also explained my inability to explain it or get anybody to believe it.

Bob listened attentively, and then began to help me in ways most people couldn't begin to understand. He strongly suggested that we needed to contact the right people, so the world could know of my discovery. I know this sounds like the same old Bob, taking charge and taking chances, but since the Love-Light-Energy experience was so genuine, Bob was making a good deal of sense.

As Bob continued, he explained a strategy with two distinct parts. While I continued to tell the campus faculty and students about my discovery, Bob would work discreetly to contact a much wider audience.

Since he was living with me again, it was easy to discuss our activities during the day and keep each other company at night, thus overcoming my unbearable loneliness. Now, with Bob's creative enthusiasm and support, the secret was shared and more likely to be explained effectively.

For my part, I did exactly as I was supposed to do. I managed to change my schedule, so I could continue to work on my degree, and altered my routine to accommodate Bob. Each night, as we shared our thoughts, Bob described his efforts to tell my story in his own unique way. To be sure, Bob described many awkward situations that developed, like when he begged for money, walked in on classes, and interrupted faculty meetings. However, there were also truly memorable moments.

For example, one especially understanding professor, who let Bob help me finish an incomplete, asked about his father living in Estonia. Bob told him that Estonia would be free sometime after the Soviet Union fell. At that time, 1980, the Soviet Union still existed. So, sometimes Bob would indeed have moments of insight and inspiration. (The Soviet Union ceased to exist on December 25, 1991)

In fact, in some ways, Bob's efforts were truly astonishing. While in one sense, it is impossible to accurately describe these activities in a coherent manner, they are certainly helpful in portraying his creativity.

Perhaps the best way to explain Bob's method of discovery is to divide it into several categories: observance of rituals, obsessions with housework, compulsions with rock songs and TV programs, and unusual use of music and television. These creative nonviolent strategies were Bob's typical methods for reaching the outside world with our story. While Bob was the one responsible for the discovery and application of these strategies, I often willingly assisted him. Not just because I trusted him, but because I also had a genuine revelation as my source of faith. Perhaps my desire to teach or my wish for fame was the source of my enthusiasm, I'm not really sure. Yet beyond my pride and gathering delusion was a sense of a new beginning.

A Strange Quest For Fame

Bob's initial strategy to spread the news about our discovery involved a kind of "creativity in actions," through which Bob tracked various objects and ideas in unique ways in order to get the attention of important people, especially rock stars. Although it is impossible to describe these activities with complete accuracy - because it is a description and not the activity itself - I'll do my best to explain Bob's behavior.

The objects Bob tracked varied according to their availability. Moving through his own intuitive state of mind, he followed many signs and symbols both at home and in the outside world. Some of the reassuring signs were: white feathers, the numbers seven and nine, license plate letters, specific times, rock-n-roll album jackets, and certain circumstances occurring around Bob's movements.

Conversely, some of the ominous signs Bob might encounter included: black feathers, the number six, the color red, the circumstances occurring around Bob's searching, and certain rock-n-roll lyrics.

In addition, Bob read any street sign and scrap of paper that he found as a way to gather clues about which way to go. Because Bob was trying to get attention from the "right people," he considered the ritual a kind of worship that needed to be practiced until he sensed that it was thoroughly and reverently completed, so as to please God.

To put the ritual in motion, let's suppose Bob wanted to follow the wind on any given day to create a "secret communication" that God and others would understand. As he walks out the door, the wind might brush against his jacket slightly to the left. Bob would then follow to the left while also watching for promising and ominous signs. As he is moving left, he notices a tiny white feather on a sidewalk by a bridge, so he crosses it. When he reaches a street called Penny Lane (a real street), he walks down that road because it is the name of a Beatles song. Bob then avoids Sixth Street, but walks down Seventh Street. He stops. The wind nudges his jacket to the right, so Bob goes right, where he sees a scrap of paper and finds the winning lottery number on the first page - 6686. He drops the paper scrap and moves on without reading any more of it. As Bob climbs over a hill, some cheerleaders cross his path on the way to the stadium. Perhaps, Bob believes, they will remember his mission as they cheer for him during the big game.

For many hours, Bob walks through the town - on streets, through backyards, and in bars. Always looking for clues, the ritualistic process will not end until Bob finds something so extraordinary that it clearly indicates that God is pleased with Bob's ritual and will grant his request. Then the quest ends.

On one such occasion, Bob was able to finish his ritual when he found an adult cow bone. It was so large he thought it was a dinosaur bone. I saw the bone myself. It was almost three feet long and was very thick. So to complete the ritual, Bob threw the bone into a nearby dumpster. For Bob, this act completed the worship and helped him to believe that now God would help us both find the rock stars who were trying to find us.

The second method of discovery concerned Bob's obsession with housecleaning; it so fascinated me; I decided to help him. This obsession included playing the B side of the album *London Town* by Paul McCartney and Wings. He played the side repeatedly. Bob began playing the album in the early morning and began cleaning the apartment very, very thoroughly. He also threw away anything he considered "unholy."

When Bob was finished, he believed that his "penance" or "offering" was acceptable, so he sat down quietly against the stark white dining room walls. Bob sat and waited for a long time, as he listened to the lyrics of the songs.

Finally, Bob realized that now he had to set the apartment back the way it was originally, and clean the house yet again. He knew the job must be done quickly, but he didn't know why. At last, as he finally swept up the last tiny speck of dirt, he realized it was midnight. Bob looked on the wall; he saw his shadow as the song played "and the grey goose flew away." He knew then, in his mind, that the housecleaning was over and unsuccessful.

Needless to say, when we went to bed exhausted that night, I realized that Bob had either fabricated some story to help him believe in his own importance, or perhaps Bob was "losing it" completely. I was so lonely during that time that I didn't want to find out. The only truly magical thing Bob did, however, involved the television. Since I was there with him, I can testify to its authenticity.

One morning Bob sat in front of the television while eating pasta from a plastic container. He tuned to a major network (NBC), and turned off the sound. Then he sat a few feet from the TV and played John Lennon's *Shaved Fish* album repeatedly for over twelve hours. Bob then interpreted the lyrics of the songs to fill in the plot: comedies, dramas, commercials, and especially the news.

After the twelve hours had passed, Bob began inhaling and exhaling very forcefully. When he finally got up and went into the bedroom, a half a dozen metal coat hangers shot across the entire length of the closet bar. Bob became extremely frightened, believing it was a demon, and then ran out of the apartment. I suspected, however, that Bob's energy might have done it through some kind of psychic connection. Regardless, it happened. I saw it.

By the time Bob had calmed down, he realized that we were both getting tired of each other again. We were "bouncing off each other" with our intensity and lack of success. We knew it was time for us to leave each other yet again.

But this time there were no hospitals or police. The whole story began, evolved, and then wound down. When we said goodbye, I knew that I would have to hustle to finish my master's degree, but it felt good to still be in school. I have no doubt that if it hadn't been for the extraordinary patience and genuine good will of my professors and counselors at the university, the whole situation would probably have crashed. But it didn't.

The whole experience reminded me again about Bob's need for medication and support in order to survive in an unsympathetic and unimaginative world. When the medicine is scrapped, anything can happen. Sometimes, it is very dangerous, and sometimes it seems like providence or just plain luck.

As time goes by, I become more and more committed to medicine and meditation, because I don't want to place my life in the hands of other people unless I absolutely necessary. The days of having others make life decisions for me are long gone. Thank God! Although the deeply moving spiritual experience on that summer morning is still largely unknown or not believed; I know what I know, and that's good enough.

Kindred Spirits

Graduating from the university, with a master's degree in English, gave me a sense of accomplishment and bolstered my self-confidence. Having been able to finish my studies, I felt certain that I could find a teaching position. Now that I was about to be married to my fiancée, Donna, I knew I needed to find some kind of employment quickly. Fortunately, just a few weeks before our wedding in July, I was able to find work as a vocational English teacher at a large refugee center in Peoria. At this job, I worked for the Catholic Social Service Agency. They actively sought out and helped resettle refugees from many parts of the world.

My responsibilities involved teaching vocational English as it related to machine tool operation and design, in conjunction with the local community college. This job eventually proved to be one of the most interesting jobs of my career even without Bob's enthusiastic presence.

There were many small groups of refugees that we served at that office. These groups of families and individuals came from Vietnam, Laos, Cambodia (Kampuchea), Ethiopia, Haiti, Afghanistan, Cuba, and Poland. All had many needs in common: housing, employment, medical services, and English classes. But they clearly differed in their resourcefulness and overall education. For example, some refugees were able to access the system quickly and effectively for things like transportation and educational assistance. They tended to learn English rapidly and had received some formal education in their native country. In addition, many had been citizens of responsibility and authority.

But many other refugees had no education at all. They had often been farmers and laborers in their in their native lands. Frequently, these refugees were not prepared to study even the most basic English, so work related things like blue prints and micrometers were simply overwhelming. Sometimes, they were very reluctant to try, while others simply copied the textbook word for word.

As you might expect, the staff at the refugee office often encountered all kinds of unanticipated challenges. For example, my responsibilities included making sure I had a certain number of students for every class. However, at least once a month, almost the entire class was missing. I came to find out that government checks arrived at the students' apartments on that day. They waited for the mail, so no one would steal their money.

One problem developed when a refugee couple went to the doctor and were given eardrops for their baby's ear infection. The baby remained ill for a while because the couple couldn't figure out how to open the medicine bottle. Another refugee father, disciplined his son by leaving him outside all night. He needed immediate family counseling.

Several situations were truly unusual. The vast majority of refugees had no money, and since many were considered "traitors" for supporting America, they had to flee their own countries or die. Many families, parts of families, and individuals escaped on rickety boats that were barely seaworthy. They were repeatedly attacked by pirates, seeking silver and gold, taking even belts and shoes.

By some miracle of providence, one very wealthy family arrived in America with all the silver and gold they had managed to stow away. This family immediately became one of the most important members of that nationality of refugees.

Another situation was really heartbreaking to watch - a bachelor refugee who married an American woman. After a couple of weeks, she realized that he was mentally challenged beyond what she thought was a language barrier, so she divorced him. He tried everything to win her back, even pleading with us to help him, but she wasn't interested in him anymore. He really struggled after the break-up for a long time.

There were also wonderful moments. Generally speaking, the students seemed to genuinely like me and were always friendly and courteous. It had been years since I felt truly part of a group. One night, the refugees all invited me for a special dinner. It was truly marvelous.

On this wonderful occasion, I saw one of the most touching sights I have ever seen. A former pilot, who had been severely burned in a plane crash, still had the love and devotion of his young wife. Despite living as refugees far from home, and even though her husband was horribly scarred, she still appeared to genuinely love him. I was stunned and humbled by their maturity and courage.

There was one recurring problem that seemed to disrupt and overshadow everything else at that time. Initially, Peoria was chosen as a refugee center since the job market was very favorable there. Because of this very low unemployment rate, the Peoria Refugee Center soon became an important resettlement location. Tragically, at about the same time, the major corporations in the area began massive layoffs.

Families that were earning enough money to afford a nice house, two cars, and college tuition for their children were suddenly completely out of work. This, in turn, created a lot of resentment and even anger toward the refugee population. Especially difficult for those laid off, was the notion that these refugees should receive money and services.

The truth, however, was that the refugees had a great deal of trouble getting work themselves; they had a time limit on how long benefits would be available. The jobs the refugees applied for were minimum wage jobs like night janitor, dishwasher, or fast food restaurant worker. The thirty dollar an hour jobs were not even remotely available to them.

Before I get too preachy, these high paying jobs were often difficult, hot, and demanding and could be on any shift. I can't imagine dedicating my entire life to such hard work specifically for pay and benefits, only to have them evaporate. These workers needed to identify a source they could blame. The refugees were the wrong source, but the factory worker's attitudes were understandable.

The refugees at the Catholic Social Service Agency almost always had their own extraordinary stories to tell about conditions in their native land and their own harrowing escapes. Many of them who made their way to the United States had supported America in various wars, conflicts, and surveillance operations. Because of this, their entire families were identified as spies and conspirators. To remain in their own countries meant certain death for all of them. Other refugees were political prisoners and "undesirables" who were basically thrown out of their native countries. Sometimes, I remind myself that the early colonists in America were often described in similar terms. Finally, I try to remember that we are all "citizens of the world," and I, like them, have often felt misunderstood and unaccepted.

To be honest, there were times when I *still* liked being different and unaccepted. With Bob, for example, life seemed wonderful, even miraculous at times. Certainly, things went a lot smoother for a time, but boredom was much worse for me. So, somewhere deep in my soul, I still longed to reunite with Bob and share another quest together.

Problems With Employment Practices

I am digressing briefly to comment on the very real, often painful, prejudices that we individuals who have bipolar illnesses experience in the job market. These barriers to meaningful employment have weakened to some degree over the years, but they remain real and formidable, despite the laws and protections our government has passed.

This part of my story may seem somewhat didactic or even bitter, but it is true. It is the only way for me to clearly state the disturbingly cruel treatment of the mentally ill that still remains in the employment market.

One of the most difficult things for us to do, when trying to get a job, is the necessity of lying on the application. Although from childhood we are repeatedly taught "to tell the truth," it is simply unrealistic for individuals with bipolar issues to be truthful about their life history.

First and foremost, although federal laws are supposed to protect and encourage us in our job search, they are used, instead, to "weed us out" from the other job candidates. Many applications even invite us to write down our disorder and suggest we will be ensured equal treatment or even preferential consideration. In fact, the automatic rejection pile is our "preferential consideration."

In truth, the laws actually serve as obstacles to employment. Employers resort to their infamous cold shoulder that takes the form of never calling back. Worse yet, their weapon of choice when cornered - "We found a more qualified applicant."

However, if we lie about anything on our application, it will lead to "immediate termination."

Following the logic:

If we tell the truth, there is no chance of getting work.

If we lie, we can be fired.

So really, the only thing we can do is fabricate some things and hope we don't get caught. That is if we want to work at all.

Another problem with the application process is the dilemma of time gaps. Most of us have a number of inconsistencies in the chronology of our education and work history. Most applications usually require applicants to account for any gaps of six months or more. An explanation like "I was in a mental hospital" isn't a really good response, especially if it is true. So, I have always played the "time shuffle" – a shell game - to the degree that it explains these gaps and satisfies interviewers' concerns, without allowing them to "get to the bottom of it." This strategy has worked pretty well.

That ignorance is still widespread when employers are acting on our applications shouldn't really surprise us either. The media continues to distort and "package" mental illness to serve its own interests. The "psychotic killer" and "deranged psychopath" are prime time elements in many programs. The portrayal of mental hospitals as "lunatic asylums" in horror and sci-fi movies further reinforce the image of mentally ill people being qualitatively inferior to "real" members of society. This general ignorance of the society also contributes to the stereotypes and bigotry that is still deeply rooted in our culture.

This attitude is reflected in everything from employment to fund raising. For example, to my knowledge, there has never been a massive rally or walk-a-thon specifically for mental illness research. When a march for diabetes, breast cancer, AIDS, or leukemia, takes place, there are thousands of wonderful participants and wide media coverage. Yet, the only march I have ever witnessed for mental illness resembled the very, very, end of a walk-a-thon, as a few stragglers shuffled by.

My point is that people do not truly know and trust us, because we are either completely invisible to them, or because they are misinformed about us and fear us. So, we have learned to be two people. The person they expect us to be, and the person we truly are.

Today, even beyond the job application, a number of imposing obstacles continue to exist. For example, Bob and I have had some really humiliating experiences that still resonant in my psyche.

The first occurred after the ill-timed knife accident, when I was just beginning a new job. I was hired on as a computer key punch operator at a small steel factory, where I typed in simple programs on IBM cards.

After about a week, the boss came in and told me that he had heard about the hospitalization, and so he would have to "let me go." The boss addressed me as if he were ordering a burger at a fast-food restaurant drive-thru. I never found out who told him and why, but I do remember my mother picking me up a few minutes later. The expression on her face eased the sting of the "knife in my back."

During those years, many good jobs required a physical examination, so all those jobs were unattainable. These examinations also required a blood test, so I had to list the medications I was taking. Worse yet, was the requirement to identify all pre-existing conditions which also served as a negative screening tool for insurance. The circular reasoning that you could get insurance if you didn't need it, was in its prime back then.

I recall another time when I applied for a movie theater manager job in California that required a polygraph test. The test, I was told, was to verify my education and work experience. The very first question was "Have you ever been mentally ill?" By the time the test administrator had finished digging, I felt like crawling under a rock.

Now, I realize that many of these practices are obsolete and illegal; however, many discriminatory practices persist. Several years ago, I applied for a permanent substitute position with a major school system. I passed all the tests, acquired a substitute certificate, passed the criminal background check, and did exceedingly well during the interview. I felt especially confident about the background check because I had passed it at least a half a dozen times for other previous jobs. In fact, I was so encouraged by the overall attitudes of the administrators that I drove to the relevant schools and wrote down directions for each one. There were about sixteen schools in all.

After a month went by with no job offer, I suspected a problem, so I finally called them. They had found out about the Chevy Nova misdemeanor that was now over thirty years old. After that, they treated me like a disease. Demanding that I show proof about the incident I, like an idiot, went to the records department of the county, but they couldn't find it. The records did show that I hadn't been arrested in over twenty-five years, but that wasn't good enough for the administrators. Even if I could provide proof, they still would need about six months to deliberate. Like they were going to call me back at all... I decided to move on. I didn't even get a chance to tell them that it was all Bob's fault.

Another situation developed that same year, when I had another interview for a teaching job. Based on the horrible experience I had with the other process, I decided to be honest. It was a dumb idea. Even though the organization was charitable and seemed open and welcoming, it wasn't to me, after they "imagined" the truth. One of my close relatives was a major officer of that charity, but even he couldn't help me. When you're bipolar, it's not who you know; it's what you "have."

Beyond these specific examples, there are, I think, some generalizations about our situation that ring true.

First, if we get sick, we almost always lose our job. We are often "uncovered" and humiliated while we become a source of entertainment and gossip.

Second, we take the jobs most people don't want. Employers tend to be far less scrutinizing in their employment process, when they are constantly under staffed.

Finally, we usually end up with jobs that have a higher stress level. Ironically, people who have mental illness are often stuck with stressful jobs, less professional bosses, and an environment that creates a high rate of job turnover.

It seems highly unlikely society, as a whole, will ever truly give us the respect and support that we so genuinely deserve. One need only project the new genetic discrimination law into real practice and experience. The implications negate the well- meaning intention. Once a technology is developed, it becomes impossible to truly regulate. (Title II of the Genetic Information Nondiscrimination Act of 2008 [GINA], took effect on November 21, 2009. Under this law it is illegal to discriminate against employees or applicants because of genetic information.)

Similarly, one of the main reasons we identify famous people with bipolar issues is to make us feel worthy of respect. For us "respect" usually means tolerance or indifference.

My psychiatrist once came up with a great idea. If people who had mental illnesses were given some sort of special bandage, perhaps everyone would be more empathetic. Even now, most people see physical illness as real and mental illness as a lack of effort - deserved somehow, and repulsive. Whenever I was really mentally ill, I was mostly abandoned. However, when I was diagnosed with colon cancer, I was treated like royalty. The vast majority of people still see mental illness as the mind affecting the body instead of the organ of the brain affecting the mind.

Before leaving this section, I need to make an important point. There are always good people around. There are always people who can empathize with our problems and appreciate our talents, courage, and determination. They view us as dedicated, hardworking, and sensitive. Whether in hospitals, on the job, or in school, good people turn up and make a real difference.

My Wife, Donna

I'm guessing that by now, the reader has begun to wonder about my wife, Donna, and why she hasn't been mentioned before or since that one brief statement a few chapters ago. Before returning to my story, I'd like to write a couple of pages about our life together.

I met Donna when I reentered the university. She had earned her degree long before I had completed my master's degree studies. So, although we were together for some time at school, we often had a long-distance relationship during which time, we were seldom together.

There are many wonderful things about my wife. One of the most remarkable has been the way she has handled all the mental health "baggage" that I have had to carry. For example, I had grown tired of worrying about when to tell prospective girlfriends about my past, because it couldn't be disguised forever. I told Donna the whole story about Bob and me with most of the unflattering details on our very first date. I was very relieved when her attitude was one of acceptance and support. Even though my adult life had been so troubled and unpromising, Donna believed in me anyway.

Another wonderful thing about Donna is her compassion for others in need. She seems to be a love magnet, who attracts friends, relatives, and those left out. She has a kind of intuitive presence and selfless attitude that can solve problems without the desire to "get something for herself" out of the situation. Because of her charitable nature, Donna has the ability to forgive others, and even forget the argument and circumstances that created the problem.

Perhaps the most intriguing aspect of Donna, is her ability to see the big picture when it comes to religion. She trusts the compatibility of other religions, as easily as she supports the faith she was raised with. Unlike me, who had such difficulty in understanding that unitary beliefs flow through all major religions, Donna seemed to understand this idea almost immediately. This has helped shape the spiritual dimension of our marriage. Spirituality has brought comfort instead of conflict.

Donna has also been very good at practical things like earning a living. She has always been able to find work quickly, and over the years, many of these jobs have paid very well. This has been a real blessing because I have never really been very good at making a decent income. Up through my mid-fifties, I always tried to work. But, whenever a good opportunity to earn a lot of needed money came along, some obstacle - real or imaginary - seemed to ruin my chances. Without Donna's income we would probably be without a home, insurance, and financial independence.

Throughout our marriage, there have still been many unforeseen problems stemming mostly from my bipolar illness. The difficult ups and downs that sometimes expand into full blown episodes have created job losses, hospitalizations, and many problems that have tested our courage and drained our resources. Fortunately, for a long time, we were in counseling with a really good therapist who helped us navigate the almost impossible challenges of managing my mental illness.

No matter the difficulty of the situation, my wife, Donna, has always been there for me. She has also been able to see the "real me" behind the various masks of my bipolar illness. Her expertise in banking has made it possible for her to make a great living; and also, has given her a tremendous ability to find, understand, and complete the ocean of paperwork that comes from insurance forms, prescription issues, and household documents.

Lastly, there are a number of close relatives on my side of the family who are bipolar, so we agreed to give up on the idea of children. (I can't imagine what Donna would do if a child and I were ill at the same time.) In place of our own children, Donna stays in close contact with her nieces and nephews and helps support two children in Africa.

Beyond all this, Donna has helped me to finally accept my disability, as the world defines it, and accept Social Security Disability payments (SSDI). I have always been very reluctant to apply, but I have been discriminated against twice for jobs I would have otherwise certainly attained.

One year, I had an employer who was a "screamer." She accused me of stealing, then, didn't apologize even after being completely exonerated. (It turned out that another staff member had forgotten to sign out for the cash.) Sometimes I have also been forced to work temporary jobs for minimum wage with men half my age.

Finally, I had successful colon cancer surgery. That was the "last straw" so to speak. Fortunately, with Donna in charge, I have since received social security benefits. Now I volunteer, do chores, and write. Everything is less stressful now. I'm very grateful for the government's help and Donna's tenacity.

In closing this chapter....

First, Donna and I don't have children, so I am in no position to give any kind of advice in that regard. I would mention, however, that bipolar symptoms are very real, even in very young children. The illness is genetic, not a result of child rearing practices.

Second, I could not have led a quasi-normal life as an unmarried person. The stress and constant demands of running a household together with the need to make sufficient money to live on would have been impossible for me. (It is often very challenging for anybody.) So, I sincerely respect all those with mental illnesses who are trying, or have found a way to be independent. They are true pioneers.

Finally, throughout the rest of this book, I will continue to follow my work history and mental health challenges as they come up chronologically. Since Donna will have been with me for this entire period, we will walk the rest of the way together.

California, Back, And Beyond

While living in Peoria, it became obvious to Donna and me that after the original refugee contract was over, employment opportunities in Peoria, and even throughout the state, were very limited because of the recession. So, Donna and I set out for California and took up my brother's offer to live with him at his apartment in Redwood City.

Even there it was very difficult for me to find work. I searched for about four months while Donna remained at the apartment since we had only one car. The strategy seemed logical, but ultimately, Donna decided to look for work. She found a job almost immediately as a salesclerk in an upscale book store. After about a week, she had also mastered the bus schedule, so she could get back and forth to work.

Ironically, a few days later, I secured a teaching job at a private school for students who had been unsuccessful in public school because of behavioral problems and/or academic difficulties. It was a co-ed school with grade levels ranging from six through twelve.

I enjoyed the teaching job because it gave me an opportunity to participate in an educational approach called Mastery Learning. In this system, a student needed to score ninety percent or better on each lesson before proceeding to the next lesson. These lessons, called *steps*, covered the entire semester, so each student could learn at their own pace. The school also provided a lot of one-on-one attention and a sophisticated reward system.

But after only two years, my desire for change and the need to "move up" again convinced me that it was time to leave. At that time, the school's founder passed away. His heirs, young relatives, were quite autocratic. Their management style was the only reason I needed to quit.

Meanwhile, Donna, who remained at the bookstore for the whole time we were in California, was able to meet some famous people like Tennessee Ernie Ford (American singer and TV host) and Dian Fossey (conservationist who studied mountain gorillas). More importantly, Donna got along well with almost everyone at her work, and we sometimes visited with these friends outside of her work.

My circumstances were far more trying. I searched for work ceaselessly and went on interviews for months, before I finally found a teaching job at a Priory. As an instructor my main responsibility was teaching English as a Second Language. At first, everything went well. I enjoyed the rustic setting, and the students were very courteous and sincere. I also worked closely with the priests and brothers. But just when I thought things were going to finally settle in, Bob showed up at my job.

It turned out Bob had tracked Donna and me through a relative who had given Bob my brother's address. At first, I didn't know what to do because I wasn't really sure what he wanted. But after talking with him for a few minutes, I realized he just wanted to visit. Since we were at the Priory, I suggested we meet at the apartment, but he wanted to talk right then. So, I relented, and eventually Bob was actually able to get the principal's permission to "shadow" me for a few days.

Before long, Bob was on a first name basis with everyone, especially a long-time instructor named Harriet. Tragically, Harriet had been severely burned in a Priory arson fire. She was pretty much left alone because of her physical appearance, but Bob made a special effort to get to know Harriet over the next few days.

Then, he came up with a plan to help her. Believing he could do a "miracle" to help Harriet, Bob began to do rituals, praying that each successive ritual would transform Harriet little by little. As the day wore on, it became obvious that "everyone" wasn't going to help him. So, Bob became more aggressive and, I'm ashamed to say, shoved a student who was out of uniform.

Although Bob didn't do anything else that could be considered physically aggressive, Priory authorities called Donna and then the police. At first, the officers went after all three of us, but almost immediately realized that it was Bob, they were after. Fortunately, they didn't arrest him, but had him admitted to a mental hospital for a few weeks instead. Surprisingly, some of the brothers at the Priory wanted me to return as long as Bob didn't show up. They were overruled.

It was then that Bob and I split up for good. Even though Donna had met Bob briefly, and even enjoyed his company, she finally saw for herself that Bob was a bad influence on me. She never made any ultimatums or conditions; but I could sense her feelings of hopelessness with Bob lurking around my places of employment and interfering with our lives. So, I told Bob that it was over for us.

Ironically, Bob actually endorsed the idea. He saw how little I "understood him" and that my life was boring and naïve. But what else could I do? Everywhere Bob was, trouble eventually followed. He wouldn't follow the rules and laws of the world and was destined to live a life of segregation and misery. So, together, Donna and I attempted to "cover our tracks" so Bob wouldn't find us, but it wasn't necessary. Bob was left as a fading memory, and life again returned to normal.

Now is probably a good time to reveal the truth about Bob, if the reader hasn't figured it out already. The events in his life throughout the story are really the true descriptions of my own mental illness.

In part, I adopted this strategy because it helps make sense of the highly subjective states that look completely absurd to an outside observer. It also seemed a good way to create a sense of the episodes that feel real and immediate. Lastly, although the character of Bob was actually not a "whole" person, all the experiences were true - from Bob's point of view. Returning to my story...

I went to look for work again, but this time I was fortunate and found a teacher/counselor job at a school and group home. These were specifically created for adults with autism. These students were some of the most interesting individuals I have ever taught. Their way of life was so unique that I learned something new about them every day.

For instance, one student was completely attached to a photograph of a TV family. It gave him a great sense of comfort and security. When he misplaced it once, he became so upset that he could not stop running and crying. Having understood the source of his sorrow, we were able to help him feel better. Another student would relax every time he looked through a fire truck book. I can't remember a time when the book wasn't effective.

One student in particular, was so unusual that his behavior was an unexplainable mystery. Each night, he would turn on the shower to ice cold, then turn it to scalding hot, and then adjust the shower to reach the back of his neck. Naturally, the staff was required to supervise the student for safety reasons.

Many educated guesses were made to attempt to explain this perplexing situation, but none made much sense to me. It clearly wasn't for attention. (The usual non-explanation.) Self-stimulation also seemed pretty far-fetched as well. It wasn't until a number of years later, that I understood the student's motivation.

I was in a mental hospital and given a medication that caused convulsions for some reason. By remaining in the shower, with alternate hot and cold water, the symptoms were greatly reduced. Somehow the process helped soothe my jangled nervous system. I thought of the man immediately after my ordeal and wished I had been able to really help him back then.

Even though I really enjoyed the job at the school and group home, the pay and insurance were limited, and there was some night work. So, yet again, I quit and moved on, and even though Donna was still doing really well at the bookstore, a very traumatic event occurred that required us to make some important decisions.

Donna's mother died. Her mom had cancer for about six years before she passed, but her death was still a horrible shock. Since I was unstable again, and in no condition to travel, Donna took the next plane home. When she returned, we decided to return to the Midwest, and my parents offered to help me earn a special education degree.

Unfortunately, by the time we arrived back at the university, my mental health was even more unstable. We stayed for a couple of semesters, and I did well academically, but the initial one year to graduate, soon became two years plus student teaching. Before long, I was very discouraged, and my health failed again. But the reasons behind the illness were not my fault.

At this point, I really need to speak to the whole issue of medication. After initially refusing to take medication, I really did my best to follow through and take them as prescribed. So, why did I get sick?

Actually, there are a variety of reasons. Twice I had salmonella, and my system was completely drained and the medications were spent as well. Another time, a general practitioner insisted on giving me a prescription for an antihistamine for bronchitis that altered the effect of my other medications. Yet, another time, my life was so dreadful that I didn't care, so the prescribed medications themselves weren't helping with the depression.

Perhaps the greatest challenge of all is getting the right combination of medications as soon as possible. For me, Lithium alone is not effective enough. So, I take Tegretol for additional help in handling mood swings. In addition, I regularly take a mood elevator and anti-anxiety medications. Because of my brain chemistry, this "cocktail" has been necessary and has continued to work for many years.

Believe me, in the distant past, psychiatrists and counselors were almost always interested in raising and lowering dosages, as well as doing away with them completely. But when it didn't work - and often it didn't – none of them showed up to scrape me off the pavement.

Without the right medication in the correct dosage, life became risky for me. Racing thoughts and feelings of paranoia often left me very vulnerable and lonely. Conversely, when I have crashed, my brain has felt like two pieces of sandpaper scratching together. In the end, the whole medication issue for me is much more complicated than it appears at first glance.

When I failed to finish at the university for the special education degree, Donna's brother offered to let us live with him for a while, as I again tried to get, and hopefully keep, a job. As usual, Donna's resume and interviewing skills helped her get a job quickly, while I found almost nothing. I did some volunteer work, but the only tangible job I could find was with a parochial school as a temporary substitute. As the stress of being without work mounted and the prospects for our own home faded, I simply sank ever deeper into despair and irrationality. Instead of accepting the unbearable situation as it was, my mind (Bob) created a separate reality in which hope and meaning were manufactured.

This episode eventually became one the most important blessings of my life. It was there, at the hospital in Rock Island, Illinois that I met a psychiatrist who was both compassionate and extraordinarily wise. This doctor literally gave me a new beginning because of his ability to understand my symptoms, and his skill in prescribing medications.

By the time I was ready to leave the hospital, Donna and I had a genuine sense of hope again. Although the past had been very difficult at times, it was not merely a matter of blaming pride and selfishness as the causes for my mental illness experiences. Put simply, the medications hadn't worked very well in the past. Now things would be different. Things would be better.

Helping Others

Since I was finding it impossible to find a job in the Rock Island area, Donna and I decided to work for my parents in their hardware store in Geneva. Although it was hard work, Donna did very well as a sales clerk, and I managed the merchandise receiving department. After a couple of years, Donna found a job as a bank teller, while I bounced back and forth from the hardware store to various teaching aide positions.

I learned some important lessons during the hardware store experiences as well. First, the customer is not always right. I don't know how customers came to believe the notion that retail clerks are fair game for bullying and insulting, but it is reprehensible. This customer attitude did, however, instill patience and forbearance.

I also saw how difficult it is to run a small business. Various aspects of business management such as: payroll, taxes, inventory cost, rent, utilities, employee and customer theft etc., are all drains on profits and cash flow. Sales can also be extraordinarily challenging with fierce competition and uncooperative weather conditions. For example, it is very hard to have a "Spring Clean Up" sale in April, when there is three inches of snow on the ground.

I enjoyed working in the family business and felt secure in knowing I could return when I needed work; however, my family finally had to liquidate the business. It is nearly impossible to compete with the mega store chains that sell goods at a retail price lower than we could buy them at wholesale price. It was a stressful time emotionally and financially for a while, but now the whole experience has faded into a quiet memory, as my relatives found other things to do.

I finally landed a job that was nearly perfect for me. I was hired as a Vocational Coordinator at a Sheltered Workshop. It is more appropriately called a Developmental Training Center. These centers provide a crucial service by giving individuals with physical and mental challenges, an opportunity to work and socialize with other "clients" and the community as a whole.

As a vocational coordinator, I supervised thirty-eight work line employees and four staff members. This job had everything: production, supervision, payroll, and counseling. The employees (clients) presented a whole range of challenges requiring patience, experience, and creativity. This job also had tangible results such as clients earning a paycheck and learning marketable skills. Although the pay was mediocre, it was the type of job that I really enjoyed.

There were also some wonderful moments I still recall. A number of times I was asked to create classes during down time. So, instead of sitting around getting bored, the clients had educational and musical activities. Sometimes, I would be asked to assist someone who was really struggling. Then, all my own experiences were actually useful and necessary. I could empathize with them and even help with solutions. Most of the staff were dedicated and easy to work with. By the time I left, I had enhanced my resume, so I could successfully interview for a job at another developmental training center in Aurora, much closer to our home in Geneva.

By far, my job as a Psychosocial Rehabilitation Counselor at Aurora has been the most fulfilling work I've had so far. It was unique in many, many ways. The clients were dually diagnosed with mental illnesses and mental retardation. They had been languishing in Elgin State Hospital for many years, until the courts made this form of "warehousing" illegal. Instead, these individuals were to be assimilated into the Aurora community by working at the Developmental Training Center and living in the community in group homes.

My coworker Beth and I were responsible for up to eight adults, during the time that they were at the center. This included work activities and socialization experiences. These responsibilities evolved into working closely with psychiatrists, work line supervisors, and group home staff. During that time, I also taught a three-day crisis management course to the staff.

All these responsibilities required a great deal of knowledge and experience to foster a good work ethic and a spirit of cooperation. Over a period of six years many clients eventually thrived, some did not. Beth and I learned a lot and, I think, so did those in the program.

Despite the success on the job, I still struggled with some character problems that limited my ability to find contentment and happiness. Ever since I can remember, I have had an unhealthy need for recognition. Beyond the delusions of fame and wealth, I have always sought out praise and acknowledgement for everything I have done. Whenever I help someone, I am always aware of those around me, so I make sure others witness my abilities. I wait expectantly for praise in every relationship; this neediness is like an abyss. I remember one day when my father was praising me nonstop for at least ten minutes. When he had finished, I understood for the first time, that no amount of praise and recognition would ever really quench the thirst for attention.

Unfortunately, the opposite is also true. In the past, when I have not been recognized for my accomplishments, or if I had been reprimanded, my ego has struggled to make sense of the situation by projecting my fears and insecurities on others. The understanding of my maladaptive behaviors has helped me remain at peace in otherwise difficult circumstances. Of course, sensitivity is a mixed blessing in these predicaments for some of us. Because of the world's aggressive tendencies and acquisitive nature, it may be necessary to be assertive and open minded. Sometimes I can do it, but often I have real difficulty.

I have still been able to work at other jobs after the six years at Aurora. I have worked as a full-time teacher for four years at a Catholic school, a part time instructor at a community college, as an activity aide at a nursing home and as an activity assistant at a senior center.

As my successes diminished and my failure to cope with work environments increased, I finally have been able to receive the social security benefits mentioned previously.

My wife, Donna, continues to work in banking and has survived a number of mergers. For the last several years, she has worked at a bank that has been true to their word about not merging. Donna works very hard; she has great coworkers and makes a good living.

Before ending the story in this present time of my life, I would like to write a little bit about my relationship to God and how mental illness saved my life.

Mental Illness, Medication, & Spirituality

As I begin this final chapter, my thoughts turn to Bob, my mentally ill persona, and the many exploits we had together. I know I will probably never "see" him again but, it was his courage and sense of adventure that opened me to many unique experiences. By taking me down blind alleys and treacherous highways, my illness showed me the wrong paths, so I could find the right one, the meditative one. His creativity and sense of wonder still remain for me, a kind of connection to some ancient past that may never come again. To follow this instinct now though, in our culture of science and machines, invites only danger and despair.

I remember thinking one day, how primitive the human race remains despite the promises of science and technology. We have been on earth for possibly millions of years. Still, after all that time, we can't cooperate in any fundamental ways. Day after day, millennium after millennium, we are willing to slaughter each other by murder, war, and genocide. Isn't that a pretty good description of insanity? Maybe the world needs to try "different" for a while.

I must remain clear about the need and justification for medications. Any spiritual experiences I have had were made possible by taking medication and practicing meditation. The opposite is true as well. Even though I did have many creative experiences when I was ill, I cannot identify them as spiritual.

I have known other people who continue to reject needed medications and their lives were/are a mess. I feel truly sorry for them; however, I don't want to join them. They often live in shabby apartments or are homeless and lost. I have little doubt that many such suffering people have tried to succeed many times, often in circumstances beyond their control. If medication could help even some of them, it might help dramatically change their lives. I genuinely hope their situations improve.

If "Bob" didn't lead me to God, he did help me understand that truth was not to be found in the external world. All the adventures that led to unusual people and "exotic" places were experiences from the outside world not from deep within my soul. Like maps leading to primal forests and sparkling rivers, they continually attracted me, but did not lead to deliverance.

Rather, it was the deep inward turning of intuition that finally allowed me to cross the barrier of life beyond death. Beyond the realm of thought, past the sea of nothing, following the pull of energy, the Love and Light is All.

I haven't been "back home" for many years now. Although it is true that meditation buoyed by medication has led me through wonderful meadows of inspiration and mountains of faith and joy, the road "home" is again hidden from me. Behind the presence of the moment, I cannot breach. Maybe the memory of Love and Light is enough. To know God is Real and God is Love is very comforting to apprehend. My heart still longs to return to the moment when so many questions were answered in an instant.

As I begin walking down this "moment of the present," I don't know where I am going. Nevertheless, my faith has grown a lot even as my patience has grown but little. My bipolar mood swings have become more energy than thought, and my sense of consciousness is stronger than ever. I have often heard the statement that "Those who know, do not speak; and those that speak, do not know." But in this age of uncertainty, we should, I believe, begin to speak out, otherwise the silence may be interpreted as absence to those skeptical scientists who now so influence our beliefs and values.

Perhaps there is no final end to the journey after all. Maybe the idea that "when one merges with God, there is no return" is incorrect. Beyond my own ephemeral experience, souls far more advanced than mine couldn't have told us about God without coming back, could they?

Before I bury the ending of my story in a jungle of pride and semantics, I would suggest that beyond the mind is a spiritual intuition that, for me, offers the best chance for success for spiritual attunement. Sometimes, I can hold on to this presence for days and often times for only a few minutes. It is an open path with no landmarks or boundaries. My deepest feeling is that this presence is "home" even though I still don't recognize it yet.

Ultimately, I'm sure many readers with and without mental illnesses have their own stories to tell, many more heroic than mine. To you, I would say that God is always there, even in the darkest night. God is the "silent witness" who lives in the sky, the ocean, and in us. In the end, I believe nothing can keep us from the Love and Light for long.

Chapter 2 : MAKING DECISIONS ABOUT MEDICATIONS

Perhaps the most significant issues facing individuals with bipolar disorder involve the choices we make concerning medications. Such major issues as acceptance, effectiveness, and side effects are almost always at the center of these concerns, and usually create the greatest challenges. Often, there are vast differences in the attitudes of the families and their mentally ill relatives concerning the need for medications as well, especially when these medications are prescribed over an extended period of time.

One of the main reasons for this long, sometimes intense debate, I think, is the genuine anxiety and doubt individuals with bipolar disorder experience in regard to taking medications. Unfortunately, these feelings of apprehension are often minimized or even ignored by both mental health professionals and families. Often, medication decisions are made in emergency situations and are presented in a persuasive manner which seeks to solve the immediate crisis. The problem, however, is the individual who is ill sometimes has no real power in the decision-making process, even after the initial emergency has passed. This whole sequence of events does little to allay the individuals' genuine fears and legitimate concerns as they confront the implications of medication and the burden of a diagnosis which may last a lifetime.

Consequently, I believe discussing these medication issues from the individual "patient's" view may help to highlight their valid objections, so these concerns can be sincerely addressed, making it far more likely that the medications will be accepted as an important part of treatment and long-term recovery.

Equally important, these ideas may also help foster a greater understanding and genuine empathy in others who are involved in the whole recovery process. This comprehensive attitude change by all concerned could, in turn, help sustain a more supportive environment with genuine understanding.

Probably the most common concern and contentious issue for everyone is the individual's willingness to take medication on a regular basis. Although there are many reasons specific to individuals, there are also important explanations, common to many, which aren't always easily discernable.

When individuals acknowledge their disorder and take medication, they often must endure society's stigma and discrimination. For example, one of the most deeply felt explanations about why consumers avoid medication, is our culture's insistence in viewing individuals with bipolar disorder in moral and judgmental terms - interpreting symptoms as character flaws, personal weaknesses, or as evidence of a lack of faith.

Tragically, these widely held attitudes create a deep and lasting scar that individuals with bipolar disorder may carry with them for years. The illness itself is difficult enough to manage without the added stress of societal ignorance.

In the minds of many of us who were initially uncooperative regarding medication, the thinking usually went something like this:

If I don't accept the diagnosis or the medications, then I don't have the disease.

This, in turn, allows me to escape stigma, discrimination, and humiliation.

Of course, this logic is horribly flawed and potentially life threatening; but it is surely understandable. The point is that to accept the illness necessitates accepting all the difficulties that go with it.

Ironically, for many years, I myself, held these same questionable beliefs about mental illness. Because of my pride and sense of determination, I believed that willpower and faith could take the place of medication.

For me, by finally acknowledging that I was an individual with a bipolar disorder, I also needed to accept the primary importance of medications; and in doing so I needed to radically alter my belief system. My self-esteem, identity, and even my spirituality were also deeply affected. In addition, my feelings of self-worth and independence were constantly threatened by my uncertainties about my mental health. I felt that I was constantly cast in the role of patient, and it began to smother my identity.

Perhaps even more distressing were my thoughts about creativity and spirituality. With each hospitalization, my mind became so tangled up that I seriously doubted my imagination would ever return. Still more disconcerting was the profound effect that my illness had on my religious beliefs. Thoughts and feelings I once considered authentic as well as spiritual experiences were now diagnosed as "psychotic" and understandably my self-esteem plummeted. At that time, this fear led me to believe that medications blocked or even disconnected my links to creativity and spirituality. This gave me - what I thought at the time - was a legitimate reason for discontinuing medication all together.

Generally speaking, it has been known for years that any attitude change, such as accepting a mental illness, usually takes a long time. Even accepting fundamental changes in beliefs, for instance, such as voting for a specific political candidate or deciding on a career change, takes time to be accepted and internalized. So, it seems unrealistic to expect individuals with bipolar disorder to immediately accept their new situation, even though it would probably be exceedingly courageous and helpful if they did.

Of course, mental health professionals and families seek immediate acceptance and cooperation from those of us with bipolar disorder for a number of very valid reasons. The issue of safety cannot be overstated here. The illness is so difficult to manage that without medications, dangerous situations can evolve that are both career damaging and life threatening. Social networks can also be strained to the breaking point causing isolation, alienation, and embarrassment.

In addition, financial resources can be depleted very quickly when there is no insurance available, or when benefits run out. Since it takes time and money to correctly diagnose and successfully treat bipolar disorder, individuals and their families often go into debt for years spending tens of thousands of dollars. This only adds to the tremendous stress that everyone experiences during this difficult period of acceptance and adjustment.

Psychiatrists also seek long-term cooperation from individuals when it comes to medications. Usually, after a long and agonizing trial and error period, the appropriate medications are finally identified. When individuals stop taking their medication - as I often did even after being correctly diagnosed - the psychiatrist has to both de-escalate the crisis and carefully manage medications again. Families. who are also caught up in this repeating cycle, are also understandably deeply concerned about relapse and safety.

Yet, this whole issue about acceptance of medication goes far beyond our own personal responsibility. In fact, many of the problems individuals with bipolar disorder face are mostly unknown to others.

For example, part of long-term recovery, social integration, and economic survival require us to lead a kind of "double life." We rarely disclose our mental challenges to anyone especially employers or perspective employers. Never have I found employment or even heard of anyone who found a job by disclosing information about their diagnosis. There were also times when I was denied a job when interviewers stumbled upon my mental health background, even after I had successfully passed several preliminary background checks.

On the job applications, I believe, "checking" any box pertaining to mental illness will immediately "disqualify" a candidate from employment because the infamous "Affirmative Action" box actually serves as a red flag. Unfortunately, at this point in time, acceptance isn't a two-way street.

To be honest, for individuals with bipolar disorder, many exciting career opportunities are really not available. Often, we must take jobs no one else wants, which usually pay less, and have more stress involved. These positions usually need to be filled, so extensive reference checks are often less intrusive. It has been my experience, in fact, that people with bipolar disorder have the ability to be excellent workers but are not given the chance to prove themselves. For me, through my association with NAMI (The National Alliance on Mental Illness-DuPage) and Chipmunka Publishing, I was finally given the genuine opportunity to share my thoughts and ideas with others. In fact, it's only been since these experiences, that I've felt safe enough to share my "secret" at all outside of therapy.

Understandably, individuals with bipolar disorder who do accept their illness and persevere enough to find some kind of employment, are very reluctant to discuss their illness and medications at work. This becomes self-defeating, however, if they begin to manifest symptoms. When this happens, many of us either quit before we have a major episode, or we struggle alone and hope our medications and coping skills improve our situation. If the situation continues to deteriorate, we may then endure the "walk of shame" as we are escorted from the building while our former coworkers stop and stare. *(See Chapter 1: Problems with Employment Practices)*

Another hidden, deeply rooted obstacle that individuals with bipolar manic depression must face, if they accept their illness, is the societal notion that courage and faith are always appropriate solutions in every circumstance. These values are often rigorously applied to individuals with mental illness, but less so for people with other diseases and medical conditions.

If individuals with bipolar disorder become ill, we are accused of lacking courage and faith. If various medicines and therapies are ineffective, we are told to have more patience and more faith. If we still don't get well, it was because we didn't have "enough" courage and faith. Soon, these subtle accusations become more direct and generalized into overall behavioral themes like lack of motivation (laziness), self-involvement (selfishness), and noncompliance (stubbornness).

Furthermore, even while we attempt to follow through with various medications, society itself clearly sends us a mixed message: "If you were strong enough and had enough faith and determination, you wouldn't need the medications; but since you're not, you have to take them."

These prevailing attitudes - which I have personally encountered repeatedly - clearly demonstrate that bipolar disorder is still not understood to be a physical disorder of the brain. Even those who assert that they do recognize it as a physical illness, still often fall back on easy explanations and all too familiar stereotypes. For example, when the illness doesn't respond to treatment, the individual is often blamed for lack of perseverance and for seeking attention.

Ironically, my own experience has been that mental illness is actually more difficult to manage than other health problems. When I fractured my ankle and later broke a rib, I was very surprised to realize that my bipolar disorder symptoms were much more painful and difficult to diagnose and treat. In addition, my feelings of isolation and anxiety were intense and unintelligible to others. It was also apparent no one really understood my thoughts and feelings.

Finding the right combination of medications was exceedingly difficult. At times, being mentally ill was like speaking a foreign language that was totally unintelligible to others. This, of course, only added to my frustration and mistrust. On the other hand, with the ankle and rib, both fractures were x-rayed, diagnosed, and treated in a very short period of time. The whole process was extremely objective and easily managed. I was also treated with dignity, respect, and understanding.

This difference in diagnostic procedures is probably one of the most important reasons for individual and societal discrimination. For most physical illnesses there are a variety of tools like blood tests, x-rays, and MRI. These diagnostic techniques are scientific in approach and objectively verifiable. However, the diagnosis for bipolar disorder is highly subjective and is based on the presence of a constellation of symptoms and have recently begun to include family histories as well.

This necessitates collecting, interpreting, and diagnosing the symptoms based on sometimes unreliable observers and incomplete family records. Because this process is in some ways "unscientific," members of society create their own explanations which are rarely supportive and sometimes cruel. Strangely enough, even though there is an ocean of evidence to demonstrate that bipolar disorder does pass through families, it is still only suggested as a possibility and not considered a scientific fact.

It is this constant uncertainty about diagnosis, medication, and cooperation that makes long-term recovery so challenging. Since bipolar disorder often strikes suddenly and forcefully, it becomes a harrowing experience for all concerned. While psychiatrists painstakingly seek answers, the family can be terrified and disbelieving while the individual with the illness is very sick and often traumatized. As emergency strategies are put in place, medications are prescribed in order to at least stabilize the patient who is so desperately ill. Even when the individual begins to recover and take his illness seriously by trusting the process, there are always real challenges in fine-tuning the medications. Then, the trial-and-error process can be so frustrating that it can be more difficult than the diagnostic process itself.

In fact, it can actually take years to accurately identify and successfully treat bipolar disorder, because psychiatrists often encounter either the manic phase or depressed phase of the illness, and so don't observe the entire cycle. Understandably, they then sometimes misdiagnose individuals as having either schizophrenia or major depression. In my case, it took a nearly fatal suicide attempt to change my schizophrenia diagnosis. Tragically, by the time the correct diagnosis is finally made, frustration and humiliation of both the individuals and their families can be devastating. They may also finally give up on treatment entirely.

When and if the correct diagnosis is finally discovered, the process of finding the appropriate medications becomes an ongoing ordeal that sometimes lasts a lifetime. As brain chemistry changes and the environment shifts, medication changes may be necessary. As this painful process unfolds over time, it becomes difficult to resist the temptation to assign blame because of the lack of success with medications and symptom management. This sometimes occurs in so called "talk therapies." Although these individual and group therapies are exceedingly useful in understanding relationships, discovering thought patterns, and acquiring coping skills, they can sometimes be limiting and deceptive if they overlook the primary importance of medications and individual differences.

It is also basically unfair to require individuals and their families to assume blame for their lack of progress in their relationships, when the real culprit is the underlying biological brain disorder. Since symptoms often appear very early in life, the lack of understanding among family members can be interpreted, at least partially, in terms of the individual's symptoms and interactions within the family. This is not the same as simply "blaming" the parents for an individual's difficult childhood. In the end, when it's discovered that no one is to blame, the revelation can be enormously helpful.

This entire process, however, requires more than a submissive willingness on the part of the individual to take medication. The person must be actively engaged in finding and adjusting medications over a lifetime. A forced acceptance, based partly on coercion, is perhaps a first step; but in the long-term recovery process, a strong determination to follow through on medications is vital. It is indeed truly humbling to accept the notion that we as individuals with bipolar disorder cannot totally control our own minds because of a biological brain disorder; however, it is often an essential step in the recovery process.

This issue about constantly evaluating medications was made clear to me, yet again, a number of years ago. One of the medications I'd been prescribed for a very long period of time was identified as a possible source of concern. It was determined that I might need to go off that specific medication. Secretly, I was eager to pursue this course of action, because I believed I might be able to discontinue its use and perhaps even discontinue other medications as well. For about two weeks I felt fine, but then I began to relapse. Even while employing thirty years of coping strategies, I still became ill and was nearly hospitalized. As the situation deteriorated, I also fell back into negative thought patterns and attempted to blame various external situations, and even loved ones, as the causes for my difficult thoughts and feelings. Fortunately, the problem was resolved, and I was able to go back on the medication. This experience was humbling and disappointing; however, it did remind me how vulnerable I am without my medications and a support system.

Certainly, when most individuals with bipolar disorder do struggle with medications, regardless of the circumstances, their problems can be subtle and easily misinterpreted. Even when individuals patiently endure the trial-and-error phase of treatment, they often struggle alone. Frequently, mental health professionals and friends have a limited insight into the individual's suffering, mostly because they have no genuine frame of reference. The belief, for example, that mania is euphoric doesn't take into account other symptoms of mania including extreme paranoia that can result in totally misreading situations. Often, it is also stated that mania includes racing thoughts and the reduced need for sleep. In actuality, the racing thoughts are uncontrollable, so they create overwhelming fear and intense anxiety. In terms of sleep, it is more accurate to describe mania as the *inability* to sleep, which can also exacerbate a horrible state of mind that makes everything else even worse. It is important to note that these symptoms can lead individuals to commit suicide if they cannot endure these intensely manic states. Since professionals can't identify with the experience itself, their attempts to understand are certainly important but sometimes limited.

Even some of the more apparent obstacles that we struggle with are often largely forgotten or glossed over by others around them. In addition to taking medications as prescribed, individuals with bipolar disorder still must manage symptoms, contend with side effects, and handle the additional stress that comes with the diagnosis.

Perhaps the most important misconception, however, is the perception that the medications are "magic potions" that solve every problem. This ignores the tremendous patience, courage, and self-effort involved with coping with the illness as a whole. When the medications are given all the credit for progress, and the individual's hard work is marginalized or ignored, it is a frustrating experience. Believe me, it is a degrading and humiliating experience to work so hard at staying well with so little genuine understanding. I strongly suspect that many individuals are far less willing to stay on medications when their own self-effort is ignored. Medications make everything else possible but for many of us, but they guarantee nothing. They just give us the chance to lead a productive life.

Naturally, together with acceptance, effectiveness is a primary concern for everyone. Sometimes medications don't work well, or they don't work over an extended period of time. Tragically, for some people, no medications seem to help much despite the best efforts of all concerned. I remember, for instance, a situation that developed where I was once employed a number of years ago. There were a number of residents in an institution, who were very positively affected by a new medication that literally transformed their lives for a long period of time. Sadly, after a number of years, the same medication proved ineffective for some.

Another prevailing condition that is equally tragic is the number of young people who are occupying entire floors in many nursing homes. They have almost no independence at all, and I suspect there are often no medications that help them. This ineffectiveness of the medications is verifiable by observing residents who are required to take medications but still aren't doing well. Sadly, society labels these individuals as "chronic," and they are viewed to be responsible for their fate because "they won't take their medication." While this may be true for some, it mostly serves to appease our social conscience.

It seems clear that the solutions for medication effectiveness should be more focused on research, innovation, and compassion rather than relying on fault finding and stereotypical explanations. The fact is there is no substitute for knowledge and important medications are discovered every year. For individuals with mental illness, it has been a very long wait.

Generally speaking, however, for most of us with bipolar disorder, medication effectiveness can be described as helpful, but only as part of an overall solution. Since each individual's experience is always unique, our mental health depends on a variety of factors. In fact, for most of us, the effectiveness of our own medications can be lightheartedly compared to a jalopy that we're driving down the street. We chug along, backfire, and occasionally stall, but we still keep driving forward. Sometimes the stresses on the road itself with its cracks and potholes can also wear us down. But without the medications, we would most certainly be abandoned on the side of the road.

Together with acceptance and effectiveness; side effects, as I have alluded to before, are a major source of conflict and anxiety for individuals with bipolar disorder. Unfortunately, often this illness formally strikes in the late teens and early twenties. The medications prescribed for these young adults invariably come with side effects that directly impact some of the most vulnerable aspects of their lives. These side effects can be so socially unacceptable, in fact, that the medications are sometimes dropped altogether. For example, it is not at all uncommon for an individual on medications to gain thirty or forty pounds in just a few months. This weight gain can be very difficult to take off and keep off for any length of time. For a young person, this is really difficult to tolerate especially when the weight is often lost again when the medications are discontinued.

Some of the other significant side effects of medications that affect some individuals include: dry mouth, restlessness, stiffness, drowsiness, and lethargy. Other, far less common, but perhaps more troubling side effects also sometimes occur especially in the trial-and-error stage of treatment. The list of side effects is endless, of course, but they are real and pose a significant challenge for individuals managing symptoms, particularly when they involve long-term side effects that are, to some degree, unknown.

Beyond the physical side effects, there are social side effects that involve activities like dating, drinking alcohol, and education. In addition, the desire to sustain a long-term relationship, for example, is often difficult for those of us with a mental illness because at some point, we will have to reveal our "secret." Then the illness may become an integral part of our relationship if the relationship survives at all. Although it is certainly true that mental illness can bring couples together, it can also create a strain on them emotionally and financially. Fortunately, my wife Donna's unconditional love, support, and her ability to navigate through the mental health system has brought us closer together despite the circumstances.

The problems with relationships, however, go beyond dating and marriage. With mental illness, usually all social relationships are affected in some way. Virtually every time I became ill, I lost friends and coworkers because of my symptoms. This caused a great deal of stress and humiliation for me especially when my "secret" life became apparent for all to witness. In time, however, as I began to think about my need for recognition, I finally developed a helpful strategy for dealing with the social effects of my illness. If people don't accept or respect me, my silent response is "the heck with them." The truth is that once people get to know me, my mental challenges aren't a problem at all - unless I become ill again.

But perhaps the most insidious social obstacle of all is alcohol. It thrives almost everywhere in our culture and for someone with bipolar disorder; it is, I believe, a significant obstacle to overcome. Our society uses alcohol to celebrate virtually everything: sporting events, holidays, birthdays, anniversaries, promotions, parties, friendships, midterms, finals, victories, defeats, and even days of the week. Alcohol is almost unavoidable in our daily lives, and it can be very difficult to turn down in every social setting. Since it is a major part of our social dynamic, being an individual with bipolar disorder is made more difficult by society's relentless consumption of liquor. Sadly, Donna and I don't attend a lot of social gatherings at all anymore. (For me, it was no fun watching everyone else get intoxicated while I drank club soda.)

It is also important to note that our society uses alcohol to manage stress and for recreation as well. If individuals with a mental illness take medication, how can they be seen as weak and lacking courage when most people use alcohol to enhance self-esteem, relieve stress, and manage anxiety? The fact is that many members of society cannot do without alcohol, not only for just a day, or a month, but for good. However, many individuals with bipolar disorder who take medications don't "get high" ever. So, how do we define weakness?

In addition, it is well known that some individuals with an undiagnosed mental illness use alcohol and drugs to manage their symptoms. It is logical that if mental illnesses were more acceptable to society, those struggling individuals would be more likely to seek treatment. This revelation could also help them understand many of the underlying factors that contribute to their alcohol and substance abuse issues.

Sadly, for those of us with a mental illness, the educational process can also be a very difficult challenge with daunting obstacles and uncertainties that most other students don't encounter. Low self-esteem and managing symptoms like depression can almost always add to the already constant stresses of paying for school and earning a degree. Losing time because of incomplete and dropped classes, due to hospitalizations and long absences, can sometimes feel like an individual with bipolar disorder is having his future stolen from him. As this sense of falling behind begins to be felt more intensely, the strategy of leading a "double life" also brings doubt and alienation. Then, the almost unbearable loneliness and isolation can cause many of us to forget about school entirely.

In addition to education, one of the core issues for individuals with bipolar disorder is the timing of the onset of the disease, which I have briefly mentioned earlier. Since it usually manifests during the late teens and early college years - during the height of social involvement - it clashes with the need for independence and self-sufficiency. The maturing youths have just left home and have either gone to college, joined the military, or entered the work force. After having been supervised for their entire lives, these individuals are finally on their own, creating their own lives, and doing the things they choose to do. This includes independently establishing their own relationships, pursuing their own goals, and exploring their own beliefs.

Then the illness strikes. Almost immediately, in many cases, victims of bipolar disorder lose control of their own destiny. They often drop out of school or the military, or they may lose their jobs and apartments. They often are back home again under constant supervision. Now, everyone wants to give them advice including family members, mental health professionals, and friends. Just when their feelings of independence and self-confidence have brought hope and freedom, their world collapses around them. Suddenly - literally out of nowhere many times - these individuals are required to accept a major mental illness as an integral part of their daily lives. Every plan is then on hold or abandoned and slowly more "realistic" goals take their place. No longer in control of their own future, there is now more supervision and regulation than ever before.

The awful irony of these tragic situations is that individuals with bipolar disorder usually do need help when it comes to successfully managing their illness. So, even while they are desperately seeking independence, they probably cannot realize this goal without accepting help and counseling. Even still, it is difficult to feel empowered when medications and therapy are replacing independent initiative and self-discovery.

Furthermore, in addition to the problems of acceptance, effectiveness, and medical/social side effects; medications also impact an individual's quality of life. If taking medication doesn't offer substantive relief and help sustain a genuine sense of purpose, they are of little value. The medications may make individuals more cooperative, but they certainly don't always encourage inner growth and development, particularly when stigma and discrimination are factored in as well.

This need for hope and purpose is crucial for everyone, of course, but probably even more so for individuals with mental illness, who have repeatedly experienced disappointment and despair. Taking medication may be the vital first step required for an individual who is seeking to realize his/her hopes and dreams, but it probably isn't enough. If thereafter, the individual is still unsuccessful in finding meaningful work and supportive relationships, then medication and self-effort may seem pointless. Sometimes individuals with bipolar disorder may give up altogether until the environment becomes more promising and their courage returns.

However, even courage and a sense of purpose are not always enough. In my view, loneliness and boredom are also very destructive yet ignored as problems. It is difficult to describe without a frame of reference, but mental illness can be very isolating and provide little substantive hope. Rejection by employers, friends, and others can lead to despair at times. Even with medication, it is tragic that so many intelligent hard-working people are still unsuccessful because they have been forgotten and simply left behind. In fact, isolation and despair can lead to mental illness even if the medications are not the source of the problem.

In addition to loneliness and boredom, there are still more complex and emotionally charged issues concerning the medications themselves when they are considered as part of a long-term solution. Because many individuals with bipolar disorder are creatively gifted; they are concerned about the way medications may inhibit or "block" their creative intelligence. I will attempt to allay these fears in another chapter, but it is relevant here to briefly outline the problem.

There does indeed seem to be a significant correlation between bipolar disorder and creativity, as any internet search of famous people with bipolar disorder will reveal. Furthermore, there is a genuine fear among individuals who are considering a long-term commitment to medication that their emotions will be muted and their creative energy will be thwarted. Since self-expression and seeking truth are often very high priorities for artists and for many other people, medications represent a possible threat to artistic endeavors. As medications attempt to stabilize moods and restore thought processes, many creative individuals worry about losing their creativity entirely.

Another important and somewhat related challenge associated with medications and bipolar disorder is the belief that medications somehow stifle spiritual thought and inhibit spiritual experience. This is another topic I will return to in another chapter, but it is important to mention here because it represents another major concern about medications that individuals sometimes experience. A root cause of this concern, I think, is the belief that God and faith can ultimately cure bipolar disorder without the need for medications. This belief also strongly infers that if the individual doesn't get well - as I have already suggested - then his faith isn't strong enough. Even worse, if the individual becomes very ill, delusions are seen as real manifestations of some spirit at work. (I have had first-hand experience with this a number of years ago.)

This reliance solely on faith instead of medications has validity for some, but it is also partially based on the misconception that mental illnesses are fundamentally different from other physical illnesses. There are few people who would even suggest that someone with a fractured arm or a case of pneumonia ignore medical treatment. However, those of us suffering with mental illnesses are treated as if our disease is curable without trusting in the advances of modern science. The fact that this topic is still actively debated, demonstrates that discrimination still persists in the attitudes and behavior of many when mental illness and medication are discussed.

So, given all these problems with medications described in this chapter, why would individuals with bipolar disorder be willing to take medications at all? Even more importantly, why would they agree to take these medications over an extended period of time? At first glance, the evidence seems overwhelming that the risks are too great, and that the benefits are hardly worth the effort.

Fortunately, there are many excellent reasons for including medications as an integral part of an overall long-term recovery strategy. To begin with, it is absolutely essential to realize that bipolar disorder is a physical disorder of the brain, and our illness is not our fault. Although it is true that we must inevitably take responsibility for it, it isn't something we caused or "deserve." Despite society's mistaken notions and attitudes, it is a genetic disease that is simply not the result of any character flaw or weakness. Even though self-effort is crucial, the illness is no different than any other physical illness when it comes to the use of medications. Indeed, I have never heard of a doctor who advised against taking medication for serious infections, or counseled a patient to use determination alone to fight cancer. Unfortunately, many people would assert that these physical illnesses are different from mental illnesses because mental illness is a psychological disorder. The truth, however, is that bipolar disorder is really a physical brain disorder with symptoms that are manifested through thoughts and feelings. In other words, the cause is physical, but the symptoms are psychological.

This area of societal ignorance is perhaps the biggest obstacle to overcome. Many of us with bipolar disorder have simply had to ignore society and well-intentioned friends who often give bad advice. Ironically, this same society treats us like "throw away people" when we follow their advice and stop taking medications. To be candid, these well-intentioned friends are never around when we get into dangerous situations because we were persuaded that we didn't need our medications.

As for me, I take medications and have done so since my mid-twenties because they provide a vital safety net. This decision has greatly improved my quality of life as well. Ironically, by following through with them, I am very independent and make my own life decisions. Before, when I would eventually become ill, my relatives and mental health professionals would need to make all my decisions, so I wasn't independent at all. For example, all my major decisions were made by others; such as where I would live, what job I might apply for, and even what medications I would take. These restrictions often led to a lack of genuine opportunity and a feeling of powerlessness.

Yet, even with all my personal strategies and coping skills to help me, medications are still vital for me. As I've mentioned earlier, the illness isn't my fault, but it is my responsibility. When I give presentations to various groups, I sometimes explain my situation using a sand castle on the beach as an analogy. I can create this castle with various techniques like: creative writing, meditation, jogging, nutrition, relaxation tapes, and inspirational reading. These coping skills are important and very valuable. However, without medication, whenever a powerful surge of thoughts and feelings crashes on to the shore, it simply washes my coping skill castle away almost effortlessly. Because the wave is so formidable, it suddenly or gradually rolls over all my elaborate strategies. In the end, when I was ill, it was beyond my control, and the illness didn't announce its arrival until it was too late. In fact, when I was ill, I was almost never aware of it until I was finally tricked or manhandled into some hospital or other institution.

The truth is simple and clear to me now. By accepting my illness, taking medications, and learning various coping skills, I have been able to radically change my life forever. This long-term recovery has also freed my wife and family from the frightening circumstances that recurred whenever I became ill. Now, I'm able to participate fully in life with the chance to learn and grow beyond the threat of losing control.

Furthermore, this long-term recovery has included the ability to remain self-confident while keeping my self-esteem intact. To be honest, one of the biggest problems with becoming ill was the need to continually "start from scratch" when it came to careers, relationships, and housing. Every time I lost a job, I had to be creative with my resume because a year and a half in an institution and halfway house don't provide marketable job references. Most relationships were strained or lost as well. Now, the medications and lasting relationships have allowed me to live a stable, productive, and creative life that is very difficult at times, but far more fulfilling than it was.

Nevertheless, the challenges with medications go beyond the will to follow through with them. There are many obstacles that sometimes appear that need to be overcome. This requires perseverance. As I mentioned earlier, by being engaged in the process, the optimal medication combinations can usually be found.

Perhaps the most obvious concern that is the most overlooked is forgetting to take the medication or overlooking the need for refills at the pharmacy. To be honest, my wife, Donna, helps me with refilling prescriptions and that has been enormously helpful. I also turn my drinking glass upside down, or check for water in it, to help me determine if I've taken the medications. Other individuals use pill dividers. Unfortunately, even honestly forgetting to take medications over time can still be very problematic.

Even still, beyond all the problems for individuals who take responsibility for their own mental health, there is still one more, little realized, yet potentially serious difficulty. This problem involves the interaction between mental health and other physical health issues. Almost always, individuals with mental health concerns have the same problems with other health care issues as most other people do. My own difficulties with physical health include a bout with salmonella. When I was so ill that I needed to be hospitalized, my body eventually purged all the poison out of its system along with the medications. So ironically, I was cured of food poisoning, but stricken with mental illness.

These examples and overall discussion are meant to demonstrate how difficult any given situation can be when medications are involved. In fact, there is so much information about medications that is impossible to explain the entire issue, especially when opinions are so divergent on the whole range of concerns associated with them. My own experiences are, naturally, subjective and limited as well, but they are lived experiences. One thing is certain; however, medications can be lifesaving tools that offer genuine opportunities for a creative and unique way of being.

Finally, I would like to finish this chapter on medications by reiterating that medications should not be seen as "magic beans" that make life easy for individuals with bipolar disorder. It is almost impossible to explain to most people the level of patience, forbearance, and perseverance needed to live a fulfilling life for those of us who live with the illness every day. Nor is it possible to describe the courage required to live with the realization that we are so fundamentally different from others. The challenges and uncertainties are daunting at times; but medication, I believe, can be a crucial element in long-term recovery that makes the journey both possible and worthwhile.

SUMMARY: 10 Observations about Bipolar Disorder and Medication Issues

1. Many members of society believe mental illnesses are caused by lack of faith, the inability to handle stress, and character flaws. This attitude may even exist within the individual himself/herself because of societal beliefs.

   ° The scientific truth explains bipolar disorder as a kind of biological brain disorder with symptoms which are mostly psychological.

   ° Since bipolar disorder is a biological brain disorder, the illness itself is not the individual's fault, but it *is* his responsibility. However, so much time is spent on stressing the responsibility part; it begins to feel like it is our fault. Then, the illness begins to feel like a punishment and humiliation, and this becomes a real problem.

   ° Since there is no definitive diagnosis or cure, bipolar disorder is diagnosed by observing a constellation of symptoms, studying genetics, and identifying how medications affect other physical illnesses. For example, Tegretol is frequently used for both epilepsy and bipolar disorder, and Risperdal is sometimes used for both bipolar disorder and autism.

2. Because acceptance of a bipolar disorder diagnosis requires a major attitude change, it is something that can't usually be embraced immediately. Far less complicated ideas, like voting for a political candidate, for instance, may require a number of speeches over a considerable length of time. Yet, individuals with a mental illness are

often required to accept a major mental illness, hastily and entirely. This can deeply affect individuals' self-esteem, identity, and even their spirituality.

° It can be very helpful to identify famous people, past and present, who have been required to accept and manage their bipolar disorder. This can often promote acceptance and enhance self-esteem.

(See Appendix: Famous People with Bipolar Disorder)

3. Often, an individual's first experience with bipolar disorder occurs during young adulthood. This is a time when independence and self-discovery are very important. Individuals are away from home, actively pursuing their own interests in school, the military or at a job. Then, usually with no warning at all, they're burdened with a mental illness, living back at home, and are given more supervision than ever. As more "realistic goals" are sought, it feels like the individual's life is being stolen from him/her.

° A diagnosis of bipolar disorder may be a life changing experience, but it also provides unique opportunities to explore the mind, enhance creativity, and overcome troubling mind states like depression.

° Although it is probably true that a bipolar diagnosis can be very challenging, it is also true that life is long and taking some time to manage the illness will bring about many benefits in the future such as complex coping strategies that are very useful.

4. Medications may make everything else possible, but they guarantee nothing. They simply give us the chance to lead productive lives. Individuals still face stigma, discrimination, and all the other

genuine obstacles associated with our illness. Medications are not "silver bullets" that manage the illness entirely. Self-effort is extraordinarily important.

° In order to avoid frustration, humiliation, and the lack of cooperation that follows, individuals need to be acknowledged for their own self-effort and perseverance.

5. One of the biggest problems associated with medications for bipolar disorder is weight gain. This common side effect creates major health concerns and formidable self-esteem issues as well. Diabetes and hypertension are genuine concerns over time, and gaining thirty pounds in a couple of months is difficult for a young person to bear. Equally important, if the medications are discontinued, the weight sometimes comes right back off again.

° Physical exercise, diet, and sleep can help manage weight gain to some degree. But for a lot of us, even with these good habits, weight gain is still troublesome. But it is also true that for most of us, the illness is much worse. It's dangerous, depressing, and isolating.

6. For some individuals, medication doesn't improve their quality of life. Either they continue to relapse, can't find steady employment, or lack any genuine sense of purpose. The medication has been promised to bring relief, but it has done little to help.

° If the medications aren't working, perhaps they're not the right ones. However, there are other possible reasons for not feeling better, such as absence of routines and lack of exercise. In addition, volunteer jobs provide excellent ways to fill the day with purpose and routine. They can also become useful references for the future.

7. Some fairly common, but less identified, problems with medications include initial bad experiences, misunderstanding of the recurrence of bipolar disorder, and the difficulty in treating the illness in some individuals.

° Some individuals are reluctant to stay on medications because they were either traumatized by a misdiagnosis or were adversely affected by a medication. In addition, some see bipolar disorder as a kind of flu that will not recur. Sadly, there are still other individuals that don't receive substantive help by any medications currently on the market.

8. The idea that medications have a negative impact on self-expression, creativity, and spirituality is certainly true for some; however, probably for most of us, medications enhance these activities because they facilitate concentration, stability, and calm. It is then more likely that daily life and relationships will remain more stable and predictable. This allows for the artist to have one "foot on the ground and one foot in the sky."

9. If a relapse occurs because of medication refusal, individuals can eventually become hospitalized anywhere, even in another state when taking a trip. Since mental health professionals in these new settings aren't familiar with the individual's diagnosis, it makes treatment more difficult. In addition, employment positions and essential relationships may be lost, requiring us to "start over from scratch."

10. To a casual observer, the idea that an individual with bipolar disorder is unwilling to take his/her medications seems irresponsible or even absurd. However, with no real frame of reference, the observer doesn't realize that they and society are actually part of the cause for this attitude.

° If individuals don't accept or identify with a bipolar disorder, then in their minds, they don't have the illness. This, in turn, means they don't have to accept the stigma, discrimination, humiliation, and all the other burdens that go with it. This includes genuine concerns about jobs, relationships, insurance, and other important life problems. Everyone wants to "fix" us. Society could help by actually accepting us and "fixing" their own attitudes.

Chapter 3 : COPING STRATEGIES - DEVELOPING LINES OF DEFENSE

Although I've mentioned coping strategies very briefly in other parts of this book, I believe it is important to devote an entire chapter to these skills because they are an integral part of the recovery process. These strategies are perhaps the one element of long-term recovery that individuals with bipolar disorder can discover on their own and develop according to their specific needs. Because of their importance as acquired skills, these strategies serve as uniquely individual contributions to overall recovery.

Even though it may be true that coping skills are sometimes introduced by professionals, they are really techniques that must be learned and practiced routinely, so that they become increasingly useful in times of stress, and when symptoms threaten to take hold.

Taken together, these coping skills form a kind of defense system providing important opportunities to manage thoughts and feelings before they overwhelm. These skills help reduce the frequency of hospital stays and greatly improve an individual's quality of life.

In essence, coping strategies represent a number of skills, that are developed over time, which address specific symptoms unique to an individual. Some examples of symptoms include racing thoughts, anxiety, and insomnia. When they appear, the idea is to employ various coping strategies to either neutralize or minimize their effects. Here are some personal examples:

° For racing thoughts, I would probably meditate.
° For anxiety, I might jog.
° For insomnia, I might try several visualization techniques.

The point is that when stress and symptoms arise, having specific tools to deal with their impact is very helpful. It is important to note that these strategies can be learned and practiced repeatedly when stress and symptoms are *not* present. In that way, the skills are readily accessible when difficult situations actually do arise.

In terms of creating these lines of defense, it is important to note that it sometimes takes years to develop an entire arsenal of coping strategies that have been proven to be effective. This is because they are based on trial and error and their benefits are different for each individual. Most individuals' preferences and lifestyles vary greatly, and these differences are essential factors in choosing and practicing specific coping skills. For these skills to be useful in a wide variety of settings, they must also be practical. For example - What happens if an individual's one main coping skill is swimming, and there is no pool or lake around? This strategy, although exceedingly valuable, cannot be relied on as the only tool for combating symptoms, stress, and medication side effects.

So, how are coping skills discovered and developed into useful techniques? Individuals can begin with activities they already do. For example, hot showers and long baths are both surprisingly helpful in relieving stress and altering moods. For me, cleaning the house, gardening, and snow shoveling almost always help me let go of anxious thoughts and misdirected nervous energy. These pursuits also help fill my day with meaningful activities, keeping boredom and loneliness from filling my mind with anxious worries. The idea about filling the day with activities is one of the most important coping strategies, and it can be defined in general terms as "creating routines."

Of all the presentations I have ever heard involving long-term recovery, the establishment of detailed routines is almost always credited as an important source of assistance. A meaningful plan for the day is often a good way to both gain self-confidence and feel a sense of accomplishment. Routines continually keep the mind engaged, so that it is not left to conjure up restless thoughts and anxious feelings. Instead of simply letting the day just "happen," so that there is nothing accomplished until late afternoon - when individuals then remember things they could have done - a specific routine begins the day with meaningful activity. The day then progresses and the mind is positively engaged. Sitting around doing nothing but watching TV or listening to music creates the illusion of activity; but since they are passive activities, neither the body nor the mind can get actively involved. It takes time and patience to develop a series of activities to create a daily routine; but it can be a powerful way to help prolong a successful recovery.

To be sure, the lack of a useful routine can lead to boredom and isolation. These in themselves can lead to every kind of mental discord - it can even threaten recovery itself. When symptoms manifest because of boredom and loneliness, sometimes medications are changed and experimented with even though they aren't necessarily the real source of the distress. Even with exactly the right medicines, boredom, loneliness, and even environmental changes can actually be the cause of symptoms.

The truth is medications can be difficult to integrate into our brain chemistry. Once the medications are working, routines and other coping skills may be needed to fill in the gap between what the medications can accomplish, and what the individual's self-effort can achieve. Although individuals with mental illnesses rarely receive credit for their self-effort, their perseverance is just as important as the medications themselves. This determination, for me and many others, has been a very crucial reason for our long-term recoveries.

Generally speaking, coping skills can be described as assisting individuals with bipolar disorder in three important ways each of which allow us to "get inside our own heads," so that we can actively manage our thoughts and feelings ourselves. Specifically, these strategies allow us to:

1. **Slow down our thoughts**

2. **Redirect nervous energy**
3. **Channel our emotions in a positive way**

Although it is absolutely true that medication and talk therapy do help, they are indirect and not under our immediate control. Medication for example, acts almost independently and individuals can "work with them," but they can't literally control them. Talk therapies can provide important ideas and guidance, but they cannot literally control the random wanderings of the mind and the infinite thoughts that can suddenly arise when no one else is around.

So, **in order to slow down thoughts** and the thinking process generally, one must manage thoughts directly. This can be done in a variety of ways; for me, *one important skill I've practiced for a very long time is meditation.* Before learning this skill, I was repeatedly relapsing because of my inability to stop my mind from churning out painful memories of the past and expectations about the future. All day long, I was constantly inundated by these unwanted thoughts and emotions, with no way to get rid of them or even redirect them.

When I began meditating for only twenty minutes a day, my mind was able to slow down long enough so I could begin to recognize these thought forms and to categorize them. Before long, these categories included past, present, and future time, as well as random imaginative thinking. This helped me understand my problems while simultaneously slowing down the process of thinking itself.

(See Appendix: A Simple Meditation to Relax the Mind and Body)

To be honest, I ignored this valuable coping strategy for years. I even ridiculed the entire concept considering the practice to be absurd. It was only after being repeatedly hospitalized and when everything else had failed, that I finally turned to meditation in utter desperation. It wasn't that the medication and counseling didn't work; it was that they couldn't eliminate the symptoms entirely. This difficult situation required that I learn effective coping skills like meditation in order to manage my own specific needs.

There are also examples of the concept of meditation being utilized in less critical situations that point to its effectiveness. For instance, parents sometimes advise their children to "slow down, take a deep breath, and count to ten." This is essentially meditation. The purpose of this parental advice is to slow down the mind and body, so the child can center himself/herself. Since the mind is tied to the breath; the slower the breath becomes, the slower the mind will function as well.

Meditation has some unexpected benefits that aren't readily apparent but are very useful in managing thoughts and moods. It aids in concentration because it focuses attention and energy; so that it can, at times, transcend the thinking process. This also expands consciousness allowing for emotional and spiritual growth. However, I must emphasize, what it hasn't done - or what it hasn't done for me - is cure my bipolar disorder or allow me to stop taking medications. Nevertheless, this meditative coping skill continues to provide me with a valuable strategy which I can use to manage symptoms.

As I mentioned earlier; in addition to managing thoughts, the **redirecting of nervous energy** is another difficult problem individuals with bipolar disorder are often forced to tackle. For many of us, it is fair to say that if our energy is not directed in productive ways, it will soon become misdirected and take the form of worry and anxiety. In other words, sitting idle for long periods of time rarely solves any problems. Instead, this lack of physical activity becomes highly problematic. The tendency of the mind to turn to thoughts of fear and nervousness is a problem for everyone to some degree, of course; however, for those of us struggling with stress and symptom management, it presents a serious risk to our long-term recovery.

Generally speaking, coping skills can be helpful in a variety of circumstances, but for generalized nervous energy, physical exercise is a most effective one. This skill can be uniquely individual, yet very powerful, because exercise seems to transform listlessness and lethargy into constructive energy which temporarily frees the individual from the grip of anxiety and depression. The practice of this skill cannot be overemphasized. Physical exercise can help elevate our mood, raise our level of self-esteem, and fend off boredom. It is not a cure in itself, but it definitely offers relief.

The problem, of course, is following through with exercising. The most important thing to consider is what specific form of exercise provides relief in managing symptoms. If some specific exercise works, then it could become part of a daily or weekly routine. This activity could also develop with patience and practice.

For me, the two most important times to exercise are when I'm feeling depressed and thoughts become anxious, and when my body is wound up and affecting my peace of mind. A lot of times I'm not "in the mood" to exercise, but I just do it anyway without thinking much about it.

Another specific area where coping skills can be very helpful is **when emotions themselves are the source of our difficulties.** Because of our diagnosis, we experience a wide range of feelings that are sometimes difficult to bear, and can be detrimental to our employment situations and relationships generally.

Emotions like anger can be very inappropriate in the work place and can adversely affect other areas of our life including friendships and family relationships. There are times when we feel *compelled* to express our thoughts and feelings, even though they would best be expressed in other places and in other ways. Since counselors and good friends aren't always available, coping strategies that help ease frustration, anger, and anxiety, can help redirect, channel, and eventually dissipate these potentially disruptive emotions. Activities like:

° journaling
° creative writing

° art

° music

° photography

These can help individuals facilitate self-expression and provide a sense of closure while also redirecting emotions toward positive experiences.

To be fair, there are often many situations in which anger and frustration are justified because of discrimination and stigma, but emotionality can make things worse. For me, my association with NAMI (The National Alliance on Mental Illness) has given me the chance to give presentations and to make and keep friends. In addition, publishing and self-publishing has given me the opportunity to express myself in creative writing projects. Anger and depression are still problems for me; but with the help of creative outlets, they are far less of a challenge now.

(For more information about NAMI, go to: https://nami.org/About-NAMI*)*

There are also many important benefits to coping strategies that go far beyond slowing the mind and redirecting anxious energy. Probably the most important advantage of coping skills is their effectiveness in keeping individuals out of emergency rooms when symptoms and stress begin to take over. Because of the self-knowledge involved in acquiring these skills, mental difficulties can often be identified and dealt with while the crisis is developing, before it really takes hold. This promotes a sense of self-confidence in our ability to manage potentially difficult predicaments while also sparing us from the mental and financial burdens often associated with hospitalizations. It also reinforces both the need and effectiveness of the coping skills we possess.

These strategies often can be beneficially generalized into other areas of an individual's life. Probably the most obvious example is physical exercise. This activity really promotes physical health, improves self-esteem and often leads to socialization opportunities. As a part of an overall strategy, exercise is certainly one of the most practical and helpful coping skills.

Another strategy that can be very helpful is developing a specific sleep routine which can be indispensable for many individuals with bipolar disorder. Lack of sleep or an irregular sleep pattern can be the single most serious explanation for irritability and interpersonal problems. Even the realization that we are tired, doesn't guarantee we'll be able to control our emotions, unless we remain quiet during these times.

The sleep pattern itself with a regular bedtime and wake-up time helps ensure that insomnia doesn't lead to racing thoughts and anxiety. Unfortunately, this rhythm of sleeping and waking is somewhat rigid and hardly promotes spontaneity, it is often yet another sacrifice many individuals with mental illness are required to make in order to stay healthy.

Fortunately, the self-discipline required to follow a specific sleep schedule, also generalizes into other activities as well which can lead to increased self-effort and patience. This, in turn, can create an attitude of resilience that may be the most important coping skill of all. These experiences provide structure and help minimize uncertainty that a lot of us have trouble handling.

These attitudes and habits are a part of a wide range of coping strategies that really represent a shift in perspective about how individuals with mental illness manage their lives. For instance, individuals with bipolar disorder almost always have at least some pent-up anger, fear, and the desire for justice. These feelings are genuine and are based on real experiences. Yet, in order to move forward in the spirit of resilience and adaptability, these feelings and memories that sometimes poison our lives must be dealt with, perhaps in counseling, and then left behind. This attitude, which can be difficult to develop, allows us to move freely into the present without all the "baggage" we have carried for so long.

The point is that good character qualities can be very valuable as coping strategies when experiences and situations become troubling. My problems with pride, anger, and impatience, for example, still affect my relationships and peace of mind; however, gratitude and humility have helped overcome my negativity allowing for alternate responses. So, instead of simply reacting angrily either mentally or verbally, there is now sometimes a space in which I can choose to control myself and so better adapt to changing situations.

Another concept that has generalized into a coping technique for me was suggested by a psychiatrist. Most individuals with bipolar disorder have vivid memories of their psychotic episodes that they have experienced. They also realize that psychotic thoughts often come and go long after the "psychotic breaks" have passed. Both these situations can be degrading and unnerving. When I discussed these concerns with my psychiatrist, he had a helpful suggestion. He explained with an analogy. He said that if one foot begins to slide away from the other, just gently slide it back. This simple idea has turned out to be very effective because it took the fear out of these thoughts whenever they would arise. This simple technique was also easily applicable for any other unwanted thoughts that would inevitably bubble up in my mind.

Another coping suggestion addresses the problems of introversion that so often affects those of us with a mental illness. Because our thoughts and feelings are so unruly at times, we tend to isolate ourselves from others for some understandable reasons. This isolation is not caused by selfishness or indifference, however. Generally, it is because we are constantly monitoring and managing symptoms that take precedent during these times. Other times we may isolate ourselves because we have had a prior lack of success in relationships and/or there are few activities that genuinely interest us.

Many of the problematic thoughts and emotions associated with bipolar disorder can lead to uncertainty when it comes to our responses to those around us. It can be extraordinarily challenging to understand the verbal and nonverbal behavior of ourselves and others when symptoms arise. The creation of specific ways to handle these difficult situations can sometimes make the difference between whether an individual sustains a long-term recovery or relapses.

Possibly the most obvious, yet most frightening, solution to this isolation is to metaphorically "dive in." Since introversion is almost always unadvisable long-term, this strategy helps individuals express their ideas and hopefully, after some success in a positive environment, they will find a measure of hope, purpose, and self-confidence.

Furthermore, fears and anxieties may decrease when individuals become less preoccupied with their own thoughts and emotions. By joining others, we "take a vacation from ourselves" which may help redirect our attention.

In addition, this introversion that also produces loneliness, boredom, and anxiety, is a state of mind that is rarely advisable as a long-term coping technique. Getting involved with activities that are genuinely interesting can be instrumental in the process of recovery. It is probably true that everyone is motivated by something. When that something is discovered, it can be a good place to start.

An important and very helpful coping technique that is usually overlooked is playing music to relax and inspire. Since ancient times, music has been an integral part of society. Since it is available in so many forms today, it is often ignored or underestimated as a possible source of relief for individuals suffering with bipolar disorder.

Since the aim of almost all musical composition is to create certain moods within the minds of the listener, it follows that music can help relieve anxiety, help lift depressive moods, and even enhance creativity. For some, New Age music is very helpful; for others Classical music is reassuring. Basically, many kinds of music may be useful in improving an individual's mood especially when it is played in order to enrich ongoing creative and social activities.

Of course, the converse is also true. Music that is meant to create a feeling of melancholy or even despair may also affect thoughts and feelings. When I was young, for example, I sometimes listened to depressing songs repeatedly, and this inevitably led to withdrawal and depression.

This paradox concerning music is important to understand because individuals can unwittingly be exposed to any type of music for extended periods of time with unanticipated results. However, once individuals with bipolar disorder identify what kinds of music affect them and in what way, music can be part of their defense system and become an added coping tool. It can serve as a source of comfort in the form of relaxation and as a backdrop for creative inspiration.

For me, and for many other individuals, it is the study of famous people in history who have struggled with bipolar disorder that provides the greatest sense of hope. By studying the lives of famous men and women who have been stricken with a mental illness, many of us find courage and inspiration. We learn to overcome society's discrimination and distrust by prevailing over their ignorance with our own feelings of dignity and self-worth.

Not surprisingly, mental illness has been so condemned throughout history that it often takes a little digging to discover how deeply affected these historical figures were by their illnesses and how they managed to excel anyway. Reading about their lives can provide yet another way to cope with bipolar disorder and the stigma still associated with it. Two specific famous people, Abraham Lincoln and Saint Francis of Assisi, are two good examples.

Abraham Lincoln sometimes had serious bouts of what can only be described as clinical depression. As a young man, when his girlfriend died, he was found in the woods with a rifle, so his friends kept him in a "safe house" until his desperate mood passed. Later, when he was president, he never carried a gun because he was afraid he'd use it on himself. Not surprisingly, some historians have argued that Lincoln's depression eventually made him a stronger leader.

Another towering figure who was actually considered mentally ill for part of his life was Saint Francis of Assisi. During his spiritual transformation, his mind was subject to extreme mood swings and his behavior was considered to be those of a "madman." Once he even tossed his father's possessions out on to the street giving them all away. Shortly afterward, he took off his clothes in front of the whole town. Certainly, these mental states were transitory; however, they do make the point that individuals with a mental illness can overcome and succeed despite their daunting challenges. Learning about famous people with bipolar disorder can draw inspiration and find reassurances even when society is cruel or indifferent.

(See Appendix: Famous People with Bipolar Disorder)

Before leaving this chapter on coping strategies; I'd like to discuss, in more detail, two areas in which coping skills are exceedingly important, namely in employment situations and relationships. In both these situations, a combination of coping strategies, good judgment, and common sense are often required in order to be successful.

The first strategy involves *becoming a good actor*. As almost all of us discover, eventually we must hide our illness. In general, most people are not educated about mental challenges, so they rely on stereotypes to try and understand. Because of this, we essentially lead a double life. Many people, even today, are unwilling to accept us if we have a mental illness. This fact is most obvious when it applies to employment. As I noted earlier, laws against discrimination when it comes to individuals with mental illnesses are meaningless. I, for one, have never found employment by telling the truth nor have I found work if prospective employers have found out my "secret" through exhaustive background checks.

In light of this sad truth, a couple of things, I believe, are helpful to know.

On resumes and applications, it is important to leave out any mental illness experiences. They are almost always immediate deal breakers. On applications, for instance, writing down that one was in a state mental health facility or in a halfway house hardly seems prudent.

Instead, filling in the time with something else such as a "my relative was ill, so I took some time off" seems like a better strategy. It's not a question of being honest; it's a question of economic survival. Society wants it both ways. They won't hire us, but they want us to work. By doing an exceptional job after being hired, individuals can justify their actions to themselves if they feel uncomfortable with deception.

This area of employment is another place where coping skills become very valuable. The temptation at an employment interview is to tell the truth, clear the air, and take the pressure off our shoulders. The problem is the ultimate goal is sacrificed. Unfortunately, the truth almost always frightens people, at least initially, and then the interview either ends suspiciously, or it begins to resemble a therapy session.

A support system is the perfect way to deal with the pressure. Over time this group, in whatever form it takes, can help in these critical situations.

This attitude is probably best maintained throughout an employment experience, after being hired. It is a great temptation for individuals to gossip about others even in a seemingly harmless way. Unfortunately, coworkers may also begin to "look for" symptoms after they know about an individual's mental health issues. This can lead to feelings of anger and betrayal.

Developing a reliable and empathetic support system is a good strategy, so our needs are met. It takes self-control, patience, and self-confidence to hold back from the authentic desire to tell the truth.

Fortunately, these necessary attitudes protect us from the ignorance of others.

The importance of a support system helps immensely with this secret life we are required to maintain. Friends, family, mental health professionals, and organizations can give us the understanding and freedom we need to drop the mask. Ironically, individuals with a mental illness have two jobs. *In a very real sense, staying healthy is a full-time job in itself.* At times, when symptoms and stress manifest, they become the most pressing problem in our lives, eclipsing employment and relationships. So, support groups are essential in helping us juggle both the problems of employment and the secret challenges of our illness.

Finally, relationships can be very valuable but sometimes problematic for individuals with bipolar disorder. *For me, one of my biggest challenges involves consistently misinterpreting conversations and situations that occur in the course of the day.* Frequently, more so in the last few years, I misunderstand what people say because I confuse the message and the tone. I often assume that the person is angry or disappointed with me. I agonize over whether I said "the right thing" to the other person. I also tend to misread any nonverbal behavior in the negative. Fortunately, my wife, Donna, often helps me better understand these situations when they arise.

This misinterpretation of people and events can be especially troubling when symptoms like depression, hunger, sleeplessness, and mistrust begin to appear. Also, irritability, impatience, and the desire to "finish" things can be very difficult to control when working and talking with others. These negative thoughts can create unrealistic expectations that lead to frustration and anger. It is only the most durable relationship that can survive when an individual with bipolar disorder loses control. Hurtful words can be very difficult to forgive and forget.

There is one last thing about relationships that is exceedingly difficult for individuals with mental illness. As I stressed earlier, almost everyone in our culture drinks alcohol. However, it is a problem for us because it can lead to depression, and sometimes trigger a manic episode. Since alcohol is served almost everywhere, for almost any reason, it can be difficult to resist. I try to remember that most people use alcohol as their own coping mechanism. This reinforces my own belief that individuals with mental illnesses are often stronger in will power than most of the rest of society.

To finish this chapter - the concept of "knowledge is power" is definitely relevant. Mental health professionals, relatives, and friends can often provide suggestions and support; but most of us confronted with such a major mental illness have to figure out the way forward alone at times. If indeed we are attempting to sustain a long-term recovery, then, self-effort, perseverance, and self-knowledge are indispensable.

While it is certainly true that others can be very helpful, even essential, they can't take the journey for us. The more individuals educate themselves about bipolar disorder and explore the possible coping strategies available, the greater the likelihood of success. This search for answers also gives the feeling of relief and empowerment once these coping skills begin to evolve. The discovery and regular use of these strategies can make the difference, in time, between living a life of hope and purpose, or simply "treading water" and "just hanging on."

SUMMARY: 10 Valuable Coping Strategies that Enhance Long-term Recovery

The following inventory of coping strategies can be employed as important "lines of defense" which may be useful in the management of thoughts, feelings, and moods. These skills, if practiced consistently, can also help to limit the intensity and duration of intrusive symptoms while promoting self-confidence, self-discipline, and perseverance.

1. Regular physical exercise can help manage stress and redirect nervous energy. It also promotes a feeling of being "grounded," so that thoughts and feelings are more focused. In addition, physical exercise addresses medication side effects like weight gain and lethargy.

   ° Some examples of physical exercise include: walking, hiking, jogging, swimming, biking, camping, mall walking, gym work out equipment, and exercise DVDs.

2. Coping skills such as meditation and other relaxation techniques can be a valuable part of any effective defense system, when symptoms become so problematic that hospitalizations threaten a long-term recovery.

   ° Sometimes, the difference between being admitted to the hospital and feeling emotionally secure is the regular practice of relaxation. They continually help to ease stress, slow down racing thoughts and quiet troubling emotions.

3. Specific daily routines are probably essential for any long-term recovery. Remaining active all day every day, including writing down chores and other activities, creates a sense of purpose and engages the mind, so it doesn't manufacture worry, loneliness, and boredom.

° Examples of routines include: chores such as laundry, shopping, and housework; a regular sleep schedule that helps insure a good night's sleep.

° Irritability and anxiety can seem like symptoms of a mental illness when they are actually symptoms of insomnia. In addition, a bath or shower can be a surprisingly effective way to temporarily drain away anxiety, fear, and worry.

4. Some coping strategies are actually positive attitudes that can be learned and practiced, so they become useful in a variety of personal and social settings.

° By avoiding extremes in emotions like "riding out feelings to the end," the individual can foster improved moods which can be more conducive to long-term recovery.

° Understanding that bipolar disorder isn't our fault helps build self-confidence in our interactions with others and allows guilt to dissolve.

° Learning to "forgive and forget" the many injustices we have experienced allows us to live in the present instead of brooding over angry memories and painful humiliations.

° Since stress is often a problem, procrastination is probably a good attitude to overcome. It simply adds to all the other anxieties and worries we already carry around.

5. If medications are taken for a long enough period of time, appropriate coping skills can be discovered and developed, so that they become powerful allies when needed. Otherwise, repeatedly starting over with medications makes it more difficult to learn and practice these strategies. The root cause of bipolar disorder is a physiological

brain disorder, so even with the best coping skills, the illness will possibly remain.

6. Since bipolar disorder requires such a complex strategy to manage effectively, therapists and other support systems are probably essential.

° In order to understand bipolar disorder, we must identify what it is, how it affects us, and how it affects our relationships. These can be difficult things to sort out alone.

° The enemies of loneliness and boredom can be so unbearable that they can drain us of every joy. Sometimes a good support system can be very helpful in combating these difficult states of mind.

° Because of our illness and societal stigma, navigating through the employment, health, and educational systems can be overwhelming. Counselors and other support personnel almost always have some experience dealing with these institutions, and so they can sometimes be enormously helpful.

7. One of the most valuable coping strategies is self-knowledge. Learning about bipolar disorder and continually observing how the illness affects the body and mind can be a rewarding and reassuring practice that helps keep a long-term recovery on track.

8. All kinds of creative endeavors can be exceedingly productive coping strategies because they not only provide an outlet for managing symptoms, but they also produce the opportunity for genuine artistic expression.

9. Volunteering can help fill the day with meaningful activities and offer a possible job reference for the future. Other social activities can also serve as coping strategies that help promote socialization and long-term recovery.

° Volunteer ideas include: churches, social service organizations, food pantries, resale shops, and hospitals.

° Some social activities include: museums trips, dollar store visits, coffee clubs, planned group exercises, flea market browsing, and garage sales.

10. It is important to state that coping skills are meant to be used together. In other words, by putting a few big things together with a lot of little things, long-term recovery can gradually gain momentum. These coping strategies can gradually replace old destructive habits like alcohol, drugs, and other problematic attitudes and behaviors.

Chapter 4 : CREATIVITY - LIVING OUTSIDE THE BOX

This chapter explores some aspects of mental illness that are clearly discernable as forms of creative expression. Because the symptoms of bipolar disorder can be so difficult to identify and manage, these creative impulses can be either misinterpreted as evidence of the illness or discounted entirely. Again, to be absolutely clear - when I was mentally ill, I had a lot of uncontrolled and misdirected energy that took the form of mania, depression, and delusions. The whole crisis was often so dangerous that it was sometimes life threatening. It was bewildering to my parents and to mental health professionals who were trying to help me. I was also unable to verbalize what was happening to me. It was only years later that I began to understand my illness and its creative potential.

There are indeed some creative aspects of bipolar disorder and its treatment that often manifest during an individual's "psychotic episodes," that can be useful, and even therapeutic, in the difficult process of long-term recovery. Beyond the general, almost stereotypical notion, which assumes that creativity merely helps people with mental illness express their feelings, creativity can also be seen as an essential process for individuals who need to tap into their own artistic intelligence. By identifying, controlling, and directing this creative impulse, individuals with bipolar disorder may be able to better cope with symptoms and manage stress. Additionally, most forms of creative endeavor can improve self-esteem and self-confidence, as they provide individuals opportunities to redefine their identity in positive ways.

This creativity is a major reason for our own inner journey. It is certainly true that life is a journey for everyone, individuals with a mental illness travel through life in rather unique and indecipherable ways. This sojourn of self-discovery can be very painful and lonely. This whole process is so subjective and societal attitudes so "scientific," that the creativity of most individuals with a mental illness is seen as mostly symptoms of the illness itself. Nonetheless, because this illness usually returns periodically throughout most of our lives, we must be aware of our creative intelligence, beliefs, and life styles because they are usually essential for long-term recovery.

In essence, the creative process itself can be expressed through art - writing in my case. This creativity both documents states of mind and interprets the artist's experience. This process of self-discovery helps in testing ideas and beliefs and assists individuals in understanding their lives. This journey often involves discovering new interests in books and philosophies that are considered foreign to our own culture.

For example, many seekers of various religions assert the notion that we are all God. In the West, it is fair to say that this idea is considered wrong or even blasphemous. But, for individuals with a mental illness, it provides a different way of understanding the world.

Now, I'm not suggesting that delusional thoughts during a "psychotic break" are safe or even desirable; however, these unconventional ideas do strongly infer that Western science and traditional religious concepts are often ill equipped to address the kind of creative expression they may encounter when interacting with the mentally ill.

Another way to explain the relationship between creativity and mental illness is to explore the well-established metaphor that "life is a stage" as Shakespeare once wrote:

> "All the world's a stage, and all the men and women merely
> players;
> they have their exits and their entrances; and one person in
> their time

plays many parts..." *from the play "As You Like It" Act 2, Scene 7*

The great playwright and countless others have portrayed life as a kind a cosmic drama in which we all play various roles. As life goes on, we play a number of different roles, sometimes simultaneously. Then we eventually leave the stage and take our experiences with us.

This metaphor is useful in describing individuals with bipolar disorder. Many of us create our own stories when we are ill that are disconnected from the more objective reality of daily life. In other words, we become the main character in our own narrative, and we use original plot lines, rituals, and props to help us find our way through the various chapters of "our book."

These stories can be so convincing that others sometimes unwittingly join in the plot without discerning that the mental illness is present. However, since almost everyone else doesn't recognize these extremely subjective aspects of our thoughts and behavior, we are seen as merely psychotic only and potentially dangerous.

Certainly, to a large extent, individuals in this state are clearly ill and in need of treatment. Someone trapped in their own story can have tortured obsessive thoughts and may even engage in risky behavior. These obsessive thoughts can feel as if the individuals are standing in front of a locked door while the walls are closing in. Frantically, they may search through countless mental keys attempting to discover the appropriate one to escape. Even more disturbing are the many perilous behaviors we may engage in when we are uninhibited. Reckless driving and directing traffic were two very dangerous behaviors in which I engaged.

Even after individuals recover, this deep-seated creative yearning will most likely return. Even when coping skills such as medication, meditation, and exercise are utilized, this primal need may endure. Like an invisible wave incessantly seeking some shore, this creative energy never rests for long. Unfortunately, if it is not identified and developed, it may repeatedly flood the mind, uninvited. Then, the entire cycle begins once again, and a possible relapse may be harder to elude.

Since creativity is subjective, I am discussing it in terms of my own experience. Writing is a way for me to redirect mania and delusional thinking so I don't continually "slide over the edge" into psychotic states, turning my life upside down. By writing poems and stories, I am able to carefully control and channel my creative energy without becoming overwhelmed by it. In fact, it is probably accurate to state that all forms of literature and art contain some redirected delusional thinking in one form or another. Doesn't an author writing a war epic, for example, need to imagine all kinds of dangerous people, places, and events? Isn't writing - and art in general - a way to redirect and channel all kinds of thought patterns?

The point is that when it comes to mental illness, creativity is usually addressed only in passing, if at all, and can inhibit an individual's chances for genuine self-expression and long-term recovery. This creative expression is a fundamental yearning for most of us with a mental illness. It doesn't simply go away by ignoring it. Imaginative writing and other forms of art, on the other hand, are often legitimate ways to express these creative thoughts before they become problematic. Delusional thoughts and actions manifest because of the illness itself, of course, but creative projects may be useful in redirecting these symptoms in positive ways before they threaten to become a problem.

Generally speaking, in addition to thoughts, one of the biggest challenges many of us face is the problem of managing emotions. Often, we are like blotting paper soaking up every feeling we encounter, so we feel too deeply and intensely. This makes us vulnerable in almost every situation.

Many of us also have a passion for life that constantly leaves us expecting more. Our incessant need for rapid change and our desire for excitement often lead to unrealistic expectations and disappointments. Naturally, this becomes greatly magnified when the illness surfaces and overwhelms our thoughts and feelings. These tendencies also can lead to self-absorption which sometimes leads to extreme introversion and depression.

However, when creativity is available in some form of art, these thoughts and feelings are better understood, leading to a more comprehensive strategy for managing symptoms. For example, one of the most important aspects of any artist's creative life is to make sense of existence. Furthermore, it is only through self-knowledge that an artist can really come to understand his own mind and the world around him.

Therefore, self-inquiry and even counseling can help explain these inner and outer realms in detail, so they are accessible in a variety of artistic ways. This can help create a sense of closure concerning the past and allow for a new understanding that expands consciousness as the present unfolds.

This self-expression is another reason why the "lived experience" is so powerful in creative art. The unique and highly unusual lives we are living allow for more comprehensive notions about life and what it means to be human. When these perceptions and experiences are recorded, after a time of inner reflection, creativity can become a strategy that takes us beyond our limitations and fears.

Having described some important ideas about creative expression as it relates to individuals with bipolar disorder, I'd like to discuss some added benefits of writing and creative art.

One of the most important character traits a writer with bipolar disorder needs to develop is self-discipline. In order to write, many courageous attitudes are often required including the willingness to face the truth about our illness and the ability to accept new ideas. As both witness and participant, we must also be constantly vigilant in the process of synthesizing our thoughts and feelings, as new situations arise. We must then take these unique experiences that lend themselves to artistic expression and allow them to blossom into new ideas and progressive insights that are valuable to both the reader and ourselves.

This attitude often takes an extraordinary amount of imagination and self-discipline, but it is very helpful for developing strategies that enhance long-term recovery. In time, these insights about ourselves and the world can be integrated into our daily lives helping us remain healthy and creative.

In a more practical way, this self-discipline takes the form of following strict routines as well as creating and maintaining valuable coping skills. In this way, writing can become a "way of being" and other areas of life can evolve around it. In order to write a novel, for instance, a writer must live in two worlds at the same time. In order to use his imagination freely, the other areas of his life may need to be as predictable as possible.

For me, chores like mowing the lawn and cleaning the house become ways to "ground" myself with physical work, so my thoughts are more disciplined and less scattered. In addition, habits I try to maintain - such as resisting the temptation to drink alcohol - help ensure a manic episode isn't triggered or a depression doesn't descend. Probably most important of all, I *always* try to get enough sleep. Without it, symptoms begin to appear, and I become miserable with little creative energy available.

By creating these safety nets, so to speak, I was gradually able to improve my writing and create a genuine sense of purpose that my jobs and relationships often couldn't provide. Ironically, the predictability of my environment allowed me to pursue my imaginative thoughts to a much greater degree than I ever thought possible.

Unfortunately, life is not so easily controlled. The impermanence and mutability of time usually overwhelm any attempt to order events in some rigid fashion. However, by regulating life as much as possible and limiting the number of distractions around me, a more productive inner space has slowly unfolded. In addition, using writing as a coping skill in a variety of circumstances has helped me to improve many otherwise troubling situations.

In particular, coping skills have been very effective in shaping and directing my writing process. Jogging and meditation, for example, consistently sort, manage, and control my mind, so I can pursue my writing on a regular basis. Often, the writing itself successfully redirects my thoughts and emotions and steers me away from frustration and alienation. Because my mind still remains restless and unpredictable at times, these skills help me to remain busy as well.

Essentially, the whole writing process can be exceedingly useful because it addresses so many elements of mental health. As mentioned earlier in this chapter, writing can help manage a number of problematic tendencies such as the constant desire for change, the incessant need for excitement, and the underlying need to create. For me, writing is a way to engage these tendencies in a disciplined manner so as to manage their influence.

One of the most difficult things for most individuals with mental illness to manage is the need to cope with boredom in all its forms. Because of our challenges, both personal and societal, we are often denied access to really interesting and engaging employment opportunities. Creative expression can be a real source of fulfillment even while working a job which is tedious and unrewarding. I believe creativity can help combat boredom and dissatisfaction by redirecting their impact, before they can actually trigger a manic or depressive episode.

I believe boredom and loneliness can be so unbearable that individuals with a mental illness sometimes "drift off" into mania and depression simply to escape their misery. At the very least, these emotions can be contributing factors for relapse.

I believe one reason my own delusions were so intense was because my own life was empty of all genuine meaning. The main reason "coming down" from the psychosis was so painful for me was because I was "forced" back into a life that was extremely limiting with no authentic opportunities.

Finally, I want to briefly mention three specific ideas about creative writing that are unique to my own process, but may also be useful to others.

First, I usually write on unlined paper, because lined paper has inherent boundaries and structure. Lined paper reminds me of all the academic baggage of my highly regimented school years.

Second, I never ask for opinions about my work. For most of us with a mental illness, we have been told what to think and how to act for so long, that it seems there is nothing genuinely original left within us. So instead of soliciting feedback, I ask my wife, Donna, to read my work, and she makes only supportive comments. This may sound self-serving; however, my writing has greatly improved over the years, and I don't write with the feeling that others are looking over my shoulder.

Third, my writing process involves my attitude. I try to always remember that the ability to write is a precious gift that should be used to express truth and beauty as best as I can. This attitude helps me write honestly and with a sense of sincerity.

SUMMARY: 10 Reasons Why Creativity is Such an Important Talent to Develop

Unfortunately, some mental health professionals see creativity as a kind of largely irrelevant footnote to treatment. However, for some of us with a serious mental illness, creative projects can be a powerful way to redirect our thoughts, feelings, and energy which is both therapeutic and fulfilling. Together with medication, physical exercise, and daily meditation, creativity is indispensable for many of us who are challenged with a bipolar diagnosis.

1. Creativity helps redirect our delusional impulses. So, we express ourselves in socially acceptable ways. Writing stories and poems, for example, may help channel this energy before it overwhelms. Since ignoring or burying this creative propensity doesn't insure it won't return, delusional thoughts may contribute to a possible relapse if left unchecked. The idea is to manage their impact.

2. Individuals with a mental illness don't *think* outside the box, we *live* outside the box. We have adapted to our situation in order to survive. It's been a very steep learning curve that has given us unique viewpoints and original insights. We see things that are not alike and combine them. When we're ill, we may think we're a religious figure; but when we're well, we might see a statute trapped in granite. When we're ill, we may speak unintelligibly; but when we're well, we can be very perceptive. For most of us, reality is often experimental, so often we generate original ideas.

3. Because of our bipolar disorder, we're usually required to undergo extensive therapy. We must learn about our thought patterns, repressed feelings, and conditioning experiences. We also need to understand how we interact with the world generally. The definition of good artists are those who understand themselves and the world

that they inhabit. This can be an unanticipated bonus of the counseling process.

4. In our relentless search for relief, we discover books, places, and individuals we never would have sought out which can enhance our creative pursuits. For example, by learning about Eastern philosophy, I was able to understand the concept of time as a circle rather than a straight line. This helped me to think and write from a different perspective.

5. The creativity that often accompanies bipolar disorder creates openness to experience that allows for unforeseen possibilities in ourselves and in the world around us. Before my illness, I was very close-minded and ridiculed ideas and practices I didn't understand. For example, I once believed that medication and meditation were both worthless until I desperately needed them to live a productive life.

6. A number of us with bipolar disorder have a high degree of intelligence. However, we can't handle a lot of stress, partly because of the anxiety that is often part of the diagnosis. Creativity, like writing and painting, for example, are practiced with no one else around. Working alone, we can fully engage our intelligence without any outside pressure. In fact, the only stress we usually experience is the pressure we put on ourselves. In addition, it is very difficult to find any job that has high intelligence and low stress. Creativity gives us a chance to build our self-confidence, maintain a genuine sense of purpose, and overcome boredom.

7. Creativity provides a sense of closure for me and helps resolve festering emotions and unresolved conflicts. I think about a problem, such as a terrible memory like Cook County jail; then I write about it, and I often experience a cathartic feeling of moving past the experience. Sometimes when I'm depressed, I can capture the actual feeling, describe it, and then let it go. Creativity also keeps my mind positively occupied, so it doesn't have the chance to focus on doubt, anxiety, and restlessness.

8. Those of us with a major mental illness have been analyzed, counseled, and behavior modified to the point that sometimes we feel like we don't have any genuine thoughts and feelings of our own. Creativity helps us move beyond psychological theories and labels, so we can discover who we really are. The study of psychology and the mind aren't the final word on consciousness.

9. Creativity expands awareness, because in the creative process we can grow spiritually by developing self-discipline. For example, after creating a poem or story, we may become a different, more mature person. In other words, thoughts and actions that once led to mental illness like "wrong turns" and "crash landings" no longer influence us. We have evolved to a new expanded level of understanding.

10. Creativity is a different kind of concentration that is somewhat disconnected from normal states of mind. A predictable routine as well as physical work can help balance the creative aspects of thought with the more practical ways of thinking.

Chapter 5 : STORIES

Uriel Fox And The Nursing Home Tragedy

Uriel Fox enjoyed his nomadic life. He often had exhilarating experiences even though boredom and loneliness left him depressed at times. Generally, he contentedly wandered the countryside. He usually found enough food and a safe place to rest. In addition, chances to earn money sometimes became available. If Uriel needed cash, he would work at almost any job. So, when he passed a "help wanted" sign in front of the Heavenly Hills Nursing Home, he recognized it as a potential employment opportunity.

Fox sauntered up the sidewalk, and immediately noticed that the building and grounds appeared to be run down and gloomy. He approached the front door, rang the doorbell, and waited patiently. Finally, a weary health care technician came to the door and asked, "What do you want?"

Uriel ignoring the tech's bluntness, replied, "My name is Uriel Fox, and I need work."

"Unless you're a nurse or a janitor, we're not hiring," the man replied curtly.

Uriel saw his chance, "Actually, I'm a janitor."

The tech subtly rolled his eyes and then handed Uriel a one-page job application and a pen. "Fill this form out and wait at the end of the hall," the tech muttered almost to himself.

Uriel waited until he was alone and began filling out the application. Completing employment applications had become an art form for Uriel Fox. His penmanship appeared to be flawless and his job history and references were impossible to untangle and verify. However, Uriel counted on his enthusiasm and penmanship to get most jobs. He hoped this strategy would work now.

When the administrator called Uriel into her office, she appeared to be friendly and actually seemed eager to hire him. Since Heavenly Hills appeared to need janitors desperately, she seemed to be trying to find reasons to hire him.

"Your application states that you have done custodial work?" the administrator asked reassuringly.

"Oh yes," Uriel answered courteously. "I guess I've always been a cleaner!"

"Uriel, I have to tell you," the administrator admitted, "I like you. Why don't we give you a ninety-day probation period? You can start on the third floor with our young patients."

Uriel decided not to ask any potentially risky questions that could influence the administrator's favorable decision and immediately took the job. He checked in with the third-floor nursing supervisor. She began giving him the third-floor rules and regulations.

"First," she began severely. "This is called the mental health floor and not 'The psych floor'. Second, do not interact with the residents because they are entitled to their privacy. Third, and last for now, as a custodian, you must do a thorough job every day. There are break periods and lunch schedules, but at all other times you need to do whatever is necessary to keep the third floor clean and presentable."

Uriel agreed and said, "I've always been a cleaner!"

"So, I've heard," the supervisor answered dryly.

Uriel soon discovered his custodial tasks on the third floor were labor intensive. In addition, the residents' privacy was indeed given top priority. Despite, this confidentiality rule, Uriel learned a great deal from the nurses and his own observations.

Perhaps the saddest thing of all was that the residents of Heavenly Hills resided there for many years. Their entire world consisted of a small bedroom, the locked third floor halls, and occasionally opportunities for arts and crafts a few hours a week - if the privilege was earned.

Being an outsider, Uriel could observe plenty of things on his own. He could see that the residents acted as if they were half asleep, probably because of the medication that facilitated with moods and behavior. Uriel also could see that couples would sometimes visit other patients' rooms, so staff nurses remained on high alert monitoring for pregnancies. The hardest thing of all was witnessing residents who genuinely believed they were historical figures. Their subtle agony seemed just below the surface.

There existed other conditions that also appeared to be very unusual. The smokers waited forty-five minutes, four times a day for smoking breaks. When they entered, they sat in a tiny room. Across from the smokers, a huge fan the size of an airplane engine roared during the entire break, sucking up the suffocating smoke. The staff abhorred this duty and sat wearing masks, and they tried ending the break as soon as they possibly could.

Despite Uriel's genuine feelings of compassion for the residents, he really disliked his janitorial job; both because of the work itself, and because of the lack of respect he experienced from most of the staff. They consistently ignored him or ordered him around when they wanted something. Even so, Uriel would have probably remained, but a crisis developed in the laundry room which accelerated his departure.

The laundry room seemed to be the most unique place on the third floor. Residents had the opportunity to toss their soiled laundry down a huge laundry chute. Since the chute remained open twenty-four hours each day, the residents could enter the room at any time. This largely unsupervised area is where the mysterious tragedy took place.

The tragic event occurred one Sunday morning, when a laundry company employee discovered a dead resident at the bottom of the laundry chute. Immediately, a controlled panic ensued, and the administrator asked Uriel to keep the laundry room locked. Then she called the emergency number - 911.

The police detectives arrived a half hour later. They surveyed the entire crime scene, took fingerprints, and interrogated staff. Uriel hid in the basement when they arrived and considered possible causes for the tragedy. He realized the young man's death was probably caused by one of three possibilities. He could have been pushed down the chute (murder), attempted to elope, or he wanted to end his life by suicide.

Since Uriel had forged his work experience and references, he would rise to the top of the suspect list. His decision proved to be simple. Uriel Fox abandoned his last paycheck and informally left his job. He didn't feel comfortable risking his future on another person's judgment. The police couldn't accuse him of the crime if he wasn't there to be questioned. He apprehended that even innocent people could be falsely charged.

So, with a feeling of compassion for the residents, Uriel Fox hiked down the sidewalk preparing to return to the open road. However, as he was leaving the grounds, two men ran up to him from the street. One of them appeared so excited he could hardly catch his breath. The other man presented Uriel with a card that read: The Law Offices of R & D Stuckerton. "If we find a problem you'll cash a check." Uriel took the card politely and then continued his trek toward the highway. On the way, he threw the ghoulish card in a trash receptacle.

The Secret Suffering Of The Mentally Ill

It is frequently asserted that individuals with a mental illness are more often victims than perpetrators of crime. I remember one specific situation that bears witness to this. Mary's tragic story happened a long time ago; nevertheless, it is a story of despair that still plays out today with many other people with mental illnesses. Although Mary's story is genuinely tragic, it certainly was not unique.

A number of years ago, state mental health facilities (state hospitals) were more popular than incarceration. Because of my own illness, I resided at one such facility three different times over a period of about a year and a half. It was at the commissary (the hospital coffee shop) where I first encountered Mary.

When I saw her, she was probably in her mid-twenties and appeared to be very ill. It was apparent she had been a resident for a long time. Like many of us, she could often be seen at the commissary where we spent time eating candy, drinking coffee, and smoking cigarettes.

This little store could often be a strange and depressing place. Although I sometimes felt delusional myself, I could still observe others that appeared more troubled than me. Some tried to hide their behavior in subtle ways, but most seemed almost oblivious to those around them. For example, a person might be sitting by the TV gesturing with his hands believing he was communicating with a minister or news reporter through the TV screen. Other, more tortured individuals might be seen incessantly muttering to themselves, as they shredded newspapers and matched them up with ragged magazine pages that they crammed in their pockets. Some residents fixated on food and devoured entire boxes of donuts and cupcakes without even glancing up at others around them. Several individuals might also be seen gobbling down entire jars of coffee by reaching in and swallowing the contents by the handful. Sometimes, other unfortunate people could be seen wandering aimlessly around the tables begging for food, money, and especially cigarettes. Since many residents smoked incessantly, they were always short. The store was habitually tainted with the odor of cigarette smoke and uncirculated air.

Occasionally, residents shopping at the commissary would scream in anger when something upset them. But the source of their rage seemed to be caused more from their delusions and not from any animosity. Locked into medications with notorious side effects and with no genuine freedom to speak of at all, eating, smoking, and sleeping were their only escapes. Once in a while, a resident would be escorted out of the building though - whether they were symptomatic or not.

One of the reasons for describing the residents at the commissary is to help explain Mary's actions in those surroundings. Her behavior, seen in context is, perhaps, more understandable.

Mary's appearance and behavior often stood out, even at the commissary. Her clothes looked like she had slept in them repeatedly, and her tangled hair appeared soaked with perspiration. She seemed unable or unwilling to speak, and her mouth was smeared with coffee grounds and tobacco stains. Sometimes when I entered the store, I could see her listlessly wandering around the room while swatting imaginary flies with a fly swatter. Whenever a song played on the juke box, she would slowly begin to dance for a few minutes before sitting down. Then after a moment or two, she would get up again and spin around while the music droned on in the background. Sometimes she danced with no music playing at all.

This image of Mary struggling could be both tragic and hypnotic. She had obviously been a very good-looking woman at one time. How could she have been reduced to this terrible condition? Yet the commissary existed in a realm filled with individuals who had been abandoned by society because of fear, ignorance, or indifference.

Imagine my surprise, when I returned to the institution for a second time and saw Mary completely transformed! Returning to the commissary, I found Mary sitting at one of the tables. Her blond hair was clean and pulled back, and she wore a bright blue blouse with black slacks. Her face was almost radiant with no trace of coffee grounds or tobacco stains. She seemed almost peaceful and happy, as she sat quietly chatting with several other residents.

At first, I thought this young woman wasn't Mary at all, but just someone who resembled her. However, before long it became clear that she was indeed Mary, still listening to the juke box and tapping her foot. In all the lonely places I have passed through over the years, Mary's recovery was truly astonishing. Even there in the commissary, her miraculous improvement provided me with genuine hope.

Unfortunately, this happy ending didn't last. Mary's storybook recovery was shattered by the time I returned to the institution for the third and final time. After my commitment, I waited about three weeks to "earn" my first pass again, and then I immediately returned to the commissary. When I shuffled through the door and walked past the security guard, I felt deeply saddened by what I saw.

As I waited to pay for my coffee, I turned, and over my left shoulder saw Mary again. Her appearance looked disheveled, and her face and teeth were stained with coffee and tobacco. She even wandered around the tables again with the fly swatter waving limply in her hand. Worst of all, she appeared very pregnant and looked disoriented and dejected.

Although I immediately recognized Mary this time, it took a few moments to understand her crisis and its implications. It was difficult to comprehend the causes of her misery. It is possible that Mary's condition had been brought about by some relapse, as she descended into some kind of psychosis. The stress and physical changes in her body were, perhaps, more than her fragile mind could bear. But I remained somewhat skeptical of this explanation. The more rational answer could be that another resident was responsible. However, the men and women were separated except for meals and even at the commissary, there was strict supervision. Since Mary had been doing so well and probably awaiting a discharge, it seemed unlikely she would risk it all.

As I continued to visit the commissary, I became increasingly angry about Mary's plight, so I finally asked a friendly staff member. Since he had always been kind to me, he eventually told me what happened. It took me awhile to fully comprehend his answer.

It seemed that two men had been sneaking on to the grounds and taking Mary out to dinner and to the theater. Nobody knew how long this had been happening, but eventually Mary became pregnant. Since the security staff and local law enforcement could not identify the offenders, and since the interlopers had never returned to the institution, Mary had no justice or father for her baby.

To an outside observer, this horrifying story is certainly tragic, but it might seem implausible. At that time, it was easy to sneak off the grounds, and residents would regularly disappear for several hours, or even days, until the police found them. Sometimes residents would also return on their own, because they had no other place to go. The only disciplinary action for elopement was the loss of a grounds pass for a while, but that wasn't much of a deterrent for individuals' intent on eloping.

More to the point, however, it remained fairly easy for outsiders to trespass whenever they wanted. I have visited my old "alma mater" several times in the past and have spent time drinking commissary coffee. At that time, almost anyone could drive into the parking lots and wander around for hours at a time.

For Mary, one can easily imagine the temptation of steak dinners, feature length movies and booze. This is especially true if one considers the hospital's deviled ham and cold wilted toast dinners, and the endless blurry-blizzard TV shows. In addition, individuals with a mental illness can be too caring, too sensitive, and too trusting. These tendencies aren't really valued in our culture, of course, so the kind and good are often preyed upon by those more cunning and aggressive.

In the end, it seemed obvious to me that Mary would not be able to keep her baby. I don't know, for sure, but I suppose it was "already spoken for" through adoption. Mary carried the baby to term, which was also probably the decision of someone else, a guardian perhaps. I have no idea whether Mary wanted to keep the child, but I couldn't see how she could care for it in her foreseeable future.

When I finally left the state institution for the last time, I knew I would never see Mary again. Perhaps she has recovered again and finally found her way. This is my hope. But one thing is certain. Individuals with a mental illness remain "throwaway" people who suffer in a society that doesn't understand or care about them. Because of this, individuals like Mary struggle in ways that most people can't believe or even imagine.

Chapter 6 : POEMS

The Carrot And The Pole

The carrot lashed on to the pole
    led to a hollow hope.
    The ring that pulled against my nose
    dragged me through do's and don'ts.
    The choking leash chewed up my neck
    and held me back from living.
    But every night I still come back
    to thoughts that need forgiving.

Structure

The structure of the pills and rules
    can keep emotions balanced.
    Like a box of useful tools,
    it helps the poet manage.
    Sometimes it can crush the soul
    because the structure smothers.
    Other times it fails to hold
    and only courage matters

Some Call It Depression

Some call it depression
    when life turns dark and dull.
    Others claim that effort
    can take the pressure off.
    Yet those who speak of feelings
    mostly live in books.
    Their minds believe in speaking
    with self-important words.

Shadow

A secret shadow troubles me
    and overwhelms my spirit.
    At times this shadow follows me
    but no one else can hear it.
    It robs me of all self-respect,
    so joy and peace are gone.
    Then happiness becomes an act,
    and I must play along.

Homelessness

She shoulders her burden
    alone in her pain.
    While others more certain
    pass by every day.
    Her feelings are scattered
    with no place to go.
    She seems to need shelter,
    but she also needs love.

Doppelganger

In a mind that mimics faith,
the thought wheels jump the track.
Sliding through beyond forgetting,
the inward engines grind and crack.
The world of hope begins to wither,
as the dream collapses fact.
But soon the doppelganger rises
chanting hymns with holy breath.
A magic road then glows and shines
that spread across and never ends.
Yet, in time a shackled life
closes off the hymn again.
The pilgrim who sought out the light,
must face the truth of might have been.

Manic Train

My manic train of thought and sound
raced down a magic mountain.
Providence bounced up and down,
and signs were pure emotions.
As my train lurched to a stop,
I felt the throttle stall.
When I wrestled with the cops,
they saw no train at all.

Farewell My Companions

When horses stampeded within my sick mind,
    You held my hand tightly and helped me unwind.
    When monsters possessed me and anger took hold,
    You knew how I felt without being told.
    When life was oppressive with dark thoughts of death,
    You asked me to linger and helped me find rest.
    When experts gave up and left me alone,
    You shouldered my burden and made it your own.
    My words can't express my feelings inside;
    Without your affection I might well have died.
    Although I have left you, I still hear you call.
    Farewell my companions. Good-bye to you all.
    Remember I love you and feel you within,
    Farewell my companions. My new life begins.

Crisis Of Thought

A vague but lingering voice
    followed the victim for years.
    Finally it ruled over choice,
    and a crisis of thought reappeared.
    His frustration and rage slowly grew,
    and the fear for his family took hold.
    One day in the woods, he withdrew,
    and ended his life and his role.

Hiding Within

Secrets fly out, friendships are lost
Feelings may crack or crumble to dust.
Everything changes, nothing holds on
Nothing held dear will last very long.
Seasons keep moving, day becomes night
Life is a journey that rarely feels right.
Everything rises, yet some day will fall,
Nothing can stop, until it is gone.
Dreams of the dreamer, burn slowly to ash
Plans for the future dissolve in the past.
Everything lingers, but never lives on
Anything happens when nothing is done.
God is a theory, man measures mind
Everyone follows the edicts of time.
A living breath pulses, a beating heart soars
Both serve their owner but then are no more.
Every day offers the chance to be good
Giving to others is better than would.
Greed is convention that wanders the plain.
Always it's different, always the same.
Everything matters, but nothing holds on.
Wealth and position may not last for long.
The world is illusion and nothing is real.
Now is forever, but no one is free.
Faith is believing, love is a being
Life has no meaning when purpose deceives.
Many things sparkle with hope and intent
Some things may matter but others do not.
Love is a symbol, a word in a book.
Silent and hidden, it lives in the heart.

Everything changes but nothing holds on,
Yet hiding within is love, light, and God.

Musical Moods

The dirge returns
    and the chairs are forsaken
    while patients bounce
    around the crooked chairs
    until the music pauses.
    Then a hopeful chair appears
    like an island of hope and peace
    giving life to the drowning mind
    in the salvation called finding a seat.
    But when the dirge strikes up again
    and the seats are then abandoned
    then only one wins,
    while the losers withdraw
    without a space, without a place, without a trace.

A Mile Past Despair

A lonely wanderer
    retrieves the trampled newspapers from the street.
    She gives free rein to her untethered thoughts
    and conjures up meanings beyond the pages.
    From these crumpled up pieces of trash,
    she dares to create her secret world
    In her faded shopping cart,
    she scavenges grimy cans and bottles
    while she mumbles her magical prayers
    and stares at numbers and signs.
    She sojourns the streets cursing and blessing
    depending on her encounters and moods.
    At night, she crashes behind the rusted green dumpster till dawn.
    Sometimes she gets captured and confined,
    but she refuses the pills
    that make her obese and withdrawn-
    a mile past despair
    and nobody cares

What Can It Be?

What can it be? Where can it be?
    Who is this monster that still follows me?
    Am I too trusting or am I a threat?
    Is it some weakness or is it some test?
    Maybe my feelings are too self-involved,
    Or maybe I'm lazy or just getting old.
    Can I escape from this prison of thought?
    Can I break free from my backsliding God?
    Perhaps all my questions are nothing but fear
    That twists up my feelings
    And makes me seem weird.
    Perhaps in this moment, I can free myself
    And find out some purpose
    That helps me reach out.
    But I know this monster
    That comes every day,
    So I will keep vigil and patiently wait.
    I have nowhere to run and no place to hide.
    I must face the creature before it's too late.

Merely A Subjective Experience

Stability is
merely
a subjective experience-
A series of
fleeting
inner events,
hooked
and stapled
together, then explained,
in order to
create
a nonexistent linear
time.

The Creative Impulse

A verse may come rumbling like thunder,
    or lightning may streak through some slumbering thought.
    A rhyme can appear and look like a penny
    that nobody found or thought to pick up.
    Sometimes the poem feels like a fever
    that never lets go not even for sleep.
    Like a fire that burns and ceaselessly grows,
    the poem itself must put out the flames.
    A poem can also bring wisdom and closure
    to thoughts and beliefs that still cling to life.
    Like a late evening shower, the verses stream down
    and point out the feelings that hide in the heart.
    Even recordings that play deep within
    can be seen in the poems the poet creates.
    Yet once in a while, the wind may blow in,
    and words feel like magical spirits.
    Writing themselves across every line,
    the words form the poem unaltered.
    But mainly the words come through like a puzzle,
    and memories seep in, awaken, and stir.
    However, too often the watching and waiting
    are unending searches for words that are wrong.

The 'All They Can Take' Buffet

At the all they can take buffet
    with the turnstiles of worry and fear;
    some customers stand lost in pain,
    and wait at the doors of despair.
    These patrons find tables for one
    and eat every meal symptomatic.
    While other are lively and fun,
    these loners are brimming with panic.
    The waiter takes word salad orders
    but serves up a fake kind of hope.
    The diners can see but ignore him,
    as the loner is smothered with cope.
    Yet somehow the dinner is crummy,
    and the beverage tastes slippery and old.
    Desserts cost a whole lot of money,
    and he doesn't buy life ala mode.
    He lives in a world called lonely,
    so he doesn't need to have faith.
    Finally, the patron that nobody knows
    leaves but returns to the play.

The John Lennon Show

Lennon sang and danced in the sun.
    He sings and dances still.
    Lifting the veil with the ritual,
    with only the picture-the show.
    The music is great,
    if I stay up late,
    and turn down the volume too low.
    The images pass,
    the sound bytes are trashed,
    and only the music can flow.
    When my mood is queer,
    I sit in my chair,
    and watch as the images come.
    I'm always surprised,
    at the visions I find,
    that propel me to most anywhere.
    I watch for guerillas,
    and number nine dreams,
    as the musical story line runs.
    The musical ads,
    and meaningless fads,
    are crushed by the beat of the drum.
    Projecting my image,
    in time and in space,
    I discover the future is now.
    I give peace a chance,
    and join in the dance,
    believing that love is around.
    Energy fills my head and hands,
    as the rhythm of sound rushes in.

Lost in the songs,
the truth comes along,
and creations of art can begin.
But in the storms of my mind,
deceived by desire,
I shoulder the karmic wheel.
The mantra I chant,
is merely a chance,
for my ego to turn me to steel.
Does John Lennon know the way?
I ask myself today.
He must be right,
about the light,
because his music plays.

Manic Wizard

Today the wizard actor plays,
    a role he has created.
He energizes every cell,
    and wanders streets elated.
Above his head, he calls the clouds,
    with mantras filled with rain.
Thunder and his waving arms,
    keep time within his brain.
This wizard knows the secret signs,
    in every spruce and willow.
He counts the numbers 6 and 9,
    and dances but none follow.
No one really knows his mind,
    because the world is flat.
No one feels his jagged rhyme-
    Mortals sneer instead.
As twilight turns away the light,
    the wizard checks the trash.
Scavenging alone tonight,
    he finds his ring of brass.
Back at home the TV screen,
    gives messages of grace.
Music from the phonograph,
    affirms the wizard's faith.
But mortals clothed in black and blue,
    begin to close the noose.
They come and talk of things to do,
    beyond the wizard's room.
Finally, the wizard rides,
    to an institution.

Believing wizard's ought to hide,
they make his reservation.
But when the metal door slams shut,
the wizard stands surprised.
Outnumbered by the groping cops,
he sees too late the lie.
As the wizard's vision fades,
dissolving into pain,
he waits to greet the lunatics,
and all the they survey.

Appendix

Famous People with Bipolar Disorder

Actors
Catherine Zeta-Jones
David Harbour
Richard Dreyfuss
Frank Sinatra
Stephen Fry
Jean-Claude Van Damme

Musicians
Demi Lovato
Brian Wilson
Adam Ant
Axle Rose
Mariah Carey
Jimi Hendrix
Kurt Cobain
Ozzy Osbourne
Tom Waits
Gordon Sumner (Sting)
Sinéad O'Connor
Wolfgang Armadeus Mozart
Ludwig Van Beethoven

Painters
Vincent van Gogh
Marcel Barbeau
Jackson Pollock
Elbridge Ayer Burbank
Barney Bubbles
Helmi Juvonen

Writers
Edgar Allan Poe
Hans Christian Andersen
T.S. Elliot
Ralph Waldo Emerson
Mark Twain
Tim Burton
Agatha Christy
Virginia Woolf

Leaders
Abraham Lincoln
Napoleon Bonaparte
Winston Churchill
Patrick J. Kennedy

Sources
https://olympiahouserehab.com/celebrities-with-bipolar/
http://www.famousbipolarpeople.com/

A Simple Meditation to Relax the Mind and Body

This practice:

° Relaxes the body
° Slows down the flow of thoughts and emotions
° Trains the attention to stay alert and steady

<u>Technique</u>

- Close your eyes
- Sit on a chair, or the floor, etc. – *don't lie down*
- Back straight, but not rigid or arched
- Feet flat on the floor, don't cross the legs or ankles
- Hands resting in your lap or on your thighs – palms up or down
- Fingers relaxed and open

Breathing
Normal breathing
Feel your breath as it passes through the nose to the lungs
Count your breath at each inhale and exhale from 1 to 10

Inhale silently count 1
Exhale silently count 1

Inhale silently count 2
Exhale silently count 2

Continue counting each breath to 10
When reaching 10, return to 1 and start over
There is no success. There is no failure. Just breathing and counting.

Besides counting to 10 these are common experiences:

1. Counting past 10
2. Forgetting the next number
3. Falling asleep

<u>1: Counting Past 10</u>
This is a reflex from when we first learned to count. Start again at 1.
<u>2: Forgetting the next number.</u>
It happens. As the body relaxes, breathing slows down; the time between numbers stretches out. It is during these "between the breaths" when the attention is most likely to wander. You may have dream-like experiences or even physical sensory input. Keep neutral about these experiences. Do not attach any importance to them, nor spend time pondering them afterwards. Start again at 1.
<u>3: Falling Asleep</u>
For many people the only time the body relaxes this much is when preparing to sleep.

With continued practice this will stop. After awakening, start again at 1. There may be days when you can't count past 3 or 4 without passing into a dream-like condition or simply forgetting the number. Just start again at 1. No judgement.

You are training your attention to stay alert and steady.

Be patient with yourself.

Regular practice is the key.

Also By John Frederick Zurn

Autobiographical

Mental Illness Experiences

The Promise of Long Term Recovery

Mental Illness and Transformation

Metamorphosis: From Mental Illness to Spiritual Awakening

The Jagged Edge Anthology

Spiritual Experiences

This Moment Called God

Passing Through the Dream

One Hundred Devotional Poems

Poems of Hope and Inspiration

Poems of Faith, Hope and Love

Fiction

Sojourners Through Time

The Extraordinary Journey of Uriel Fox

Northland Chronicles-Mother World in Peril

Non-Fiction: The Comedy in Everyday Life

Find these and more at:

https://www.portalstoinnerdimensions.com/

Don't miss out!

Visit the website below and you can sign up to receive emails whenever John Frederick Zurn publishes a new book. There's no charge and no obligation.

https://books2read.com/r/B-A-IHPT-UIUZB

BOOKS2READ

Connecting independent readers to independent writers.

www.ingramcontent.com/pod-product-compliance
Lightning Source LLC
Chambersburg PA
CBHW022007120726
47992CB00001B/462